Preliminaries to Linguistic Phonetics

Preliminaries to Linguistic Phonetics

Peter Ladefoged

The University of Chicago Press
Chicago and London

International Standard Book Number: 0-226-46786-4
Library of Congress Catalog Card Number: 75-179318

The University of Chicago Press, Chicago 60637
The University of Chicago Press, Ltd., London
© 1971 by The University of Chicago
Published 1971
Printed in the United States of America

For J.L.

Contents

Acknowledgments

The preliminary version of this book was called *Linguistic Phonetics*. It appeared in June 1967 in the UCLA Phonetics Laboratory series, *Working Papers in Phonetics*. Many people at UCLA offered helpful comments, notably William Bright, Victoria Fromkin, Frank Heny, Kalon Kelley, Chin Kim, John Ohala, Barbara Partee, Tim Smith, Robert Stockwell, Marcel Tatham, Ralph Vanderslice, and Harry Whitaker. I have also received useful criticisms of the original version from Charles-James Bailey, Elizabeth Dunstan, Morris Halle, Kenneth Hill, Barbara Hollenbach, Winfred Lehman, Sven Öhman, Elizabeth Uldall, and William Wang. If it had not been for all of them, a poorer book would have been published much more rapidly. In addition I owe a special debt of thanks to Leon Jacobson, who supervised the preparation of this complex manuscript, and to Jeanne Yamane, who typed it.

The work reported here was supported in part by UCLA intramural research funds and in part by grants from the National Science Foundation. Some of the tables were prepared by the UCLA Engineering Reports Group, but the major part of this work was prepared for camera-ready reproduction by the Volt Technical Corporation, Anaheim Branch.

1. Introduction

This book is about some of the phonetic events that occur in the languages of the world. The data described consist mainly of contrasts observable at the systematic phonetic level in a wide variety of languages. In many cases I have little or no knowledge of the underlying relations among the sounds in the languages being used to illustrate a particular point. Consequently I in no way wish to imply that the features needed for describing the sounds used in these contrasts are necessarily the same as those needed for specifying contrasts among underlying forms. If, for example, I had been using English to illustrate contrasts among nasals, I would have used pairs of words such as *sin* and *sing*. From the phonetic point of view it is irrelevant that Chomsky and Halle (1968) have shown that the underlying forms of these two words are **sin** and **sing**. It may well be that the most appropriate classification of the words in the lexicon of English does not use a contrast between an alveolar and a velar nasal. Nevertheless, when we are trying to describe the phonetic events which occur in the language we must be able to specify this difference. It does not matter whether or not particular contrasts occur among underlying forms; a phonological theory must be capable of specifying all the phonetic events in a language.

I do not know whether the set of features required for describing these systematic phonetic contrasts is greater than or equal to the set required for classifying the lexical contrasts in all the languages of the world. Indeed, there is no clear evidence showing that the set of features required for specifying phonetic contrasts is the same as that required for specifying the natural classes of sounds required in phonological rules. But we cannot develop an adequate phonological theory without knowing a great deal more about both the surface phonetic events and the rules governing the patterns of sounds which occur in a great many languages. This book is part of this preliminary work.

The task undertaken is to describe the speech mechanism using a traditional approach based on that of Pike (1943) and Abercrombie (1967), and at the same time to discuss the way the mechanism is used to produce many of the systematic phonetic contrasts in the languages of the world. The reader is assumed to be familiar with this traditional phonetic approach and with the symbols of the International Phonetic Association (1949). Comments on some of the less familiar symbols and notes on modifications of the IPA system are given in the legends for the tables.

Most of the fieldwork for this book has been done in conjunction with other linguists, all of whom I hope I have credited in the appropriate places.

But all the data in the tables are based on my own observations with informants. Similarly, I must accept responsibility for all the claims in the text, such as the claim that Marwari contrasts h and ɦ , or that Margi distinguishes between l and ɭ ; remarks of this kind imply that I have heard native speakers of these languages making the distinctions in the way described; and that these sounds contrast in the ways indicated, at least at the systematic phonetic level. (But it does not, of course, follow that these contrasts should necessarily be represented in the underlying phonological forms.)

Because of this predilection for basing my remarks on personal observation, this book is often inadequate in that my data are from a very limited number of speakers and a very small proportion of the languages of the world. I have investigated the phonetic structure of a number of African, Indian, and European languages, and have been able to make scattered observations of some of the prominent languages (and a few of the less well known ones) outside these areas. But there are many language families which I know only through the literature; and, as most practicing phoneticians would agree from experience, published phonetic descriptions are often impossible to interpret accurately. I hope this book will help improve the situation. But the statements made here should all be regarded as tentative; they are made in the belief that "a rule requiring amendation is more useful than the absence of any rule" (Jakobson 1962).

Using a traditional approach, speech may be considered to be the product of four separate processes: the airstream process, the phonation process, the oro-nasal process, and the articulatory process. As a first simplification we may associate these four processes with the actions of the lungs, the vocal cords, the velum, and the tongue and lips, as shown schematically in figure 1; but, as we shall see later, the act of moving a body of air (which is termed the airstream process) may be more complicated. Variations in the airstream process which produce linguistic contrasts will be discussed after we have considered the actions of the vocal cords (which are summed up under the label of the phonation process). We will then consider contrasts dependent on the states of the velum (which form the oro-nasal process). This will be followed by a detailed examination of systematic phonetic contrasts dependent on the actions of the tongue and lips (which form the articulatory process). The articulatory process is the most complicated of the four, consisting of several semi-independent subprocesses. We will follow the usual approach of considering the actions of the tongue and lips which make up this process first in terms of the possible places, and then in terms of the possible manners of articulation. Next we will consider the role of secondary articulations, which

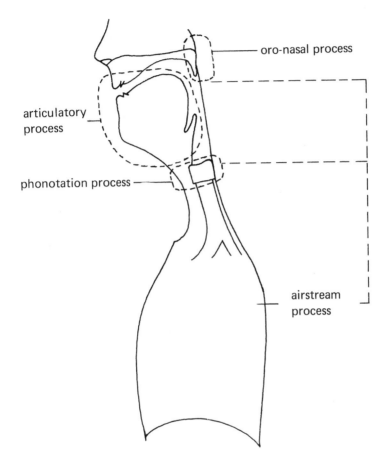

oro-nasal process

articulatory process

phonotation process

airstream process

Fig. 1. Schematic diagram of the vocal organs, showing the four processes required in the specification of speech.

are defined as those having a lesser degree of stricture, or (if there are two strictures of equal magnitude) as being farther from the glottis. Then a chapter is devoted to the description of vowels (and a few other sounds) in terms of their auditory and acoustic characteristics.

There are no immediately obvious reasons for having a chapter on the acoustic characteristics of certain speech sounds in a book of this kind. It is perfectly possible to describe all the systematic phonetic differences which occur among languages in terms of the sound-producing mechanism. But in some instances this does not seem to be an appropriate way of characterizing the features underlying the contrasts. Correct description of the position of the tongue in vowels is extremely difficult (and not as given in traditional physiological phonetic texts); but differences among vowels are fairly easy to state in acoustic terms. Similarly some consonants can be grouped together on an acoustic parameter much more easily than in physiological terms. Furthermore, although we could (with difficulty) characterize all possible systematic phonetic contrasts entirely in physiological terms, it would be ridiculous to overlook the fact that some phonological rules obviously work in terms of acoustic properties of sounds. Although the main data for this book are sets of systematic phonetic contrasts, these are not all that will be considered. Accounting for systematic phonetic contrasts is in itself a trivial and uninteresting task that can be done in many ways. It becomes interesting only when we try to constrain our account so that it fits in with the division of sounds into the natural classes required in phonological rules.

The ultimate aim of this book is to assist in the development of a set of features which would be appropriate for phonological descriptions. While surveying systematic phonetic contrasts a comprehensive set of phonetic features for characterizing segments will be proposed. For the purposes of this book it does not matter whether we follow Chomsky and Halle (1968) and try to characterize what a speaker knows about the phonetic facts of his language or whether, as I have argued elsewhere (Ladefoged 1971a, 1971b), there should be more constraints on a phonetic description, so that a greater part of it is experimentally observable. But it is important to note that we do not have the choice of thinking either in acoustic or in physiological terms. The patterns that arise in the sounds of a language are due to intersecting causes. At least two quite different kinds of features are needed to explain them. Some patterns can be explained in terms of acoustic events, others in terms of articulatory events. Thus, on the one hand, there is no doubt that p and k go together in the formation of patterns in some languages; this is because of their acoustic similarity (which used to be called gravity by Jakobson, Fant,

4

and Halle 1952), and no amount of guesswork is likely to lead to establishing anything in common in the neural commands to the speech organs which make them. But on the other hand, patterns of the kind exhibited in the formation of compounds such as **mp nt ŋk** are obviously due to articulatory constraints; and it is difficult to state rules concerning them in terms of meaningful acoustic features.

The final chapter of this book will compare the proposed set of systematic phonetic features with that suggested by Chomsky and Halle. No attempt will be made to compare their specification of what they call "the phonetic capabilities of man" with that given here until the final chapter for two reasons. First, their features are intended to take into account all the ways in which sounds pattern in phonological rules; consequently they need to define features which will divide sounds into major classes, such as consonants and vowels, which are less relevant at the systematic phonetic level. Second, their whole approach to the speech mechanism is different: some things which appear to me to be differences of phonation types they confuse with others which are clearly due to differences in the articulatory process. Consequently the two sets of features can be compared only when we have a complete description of the speech mechanism.

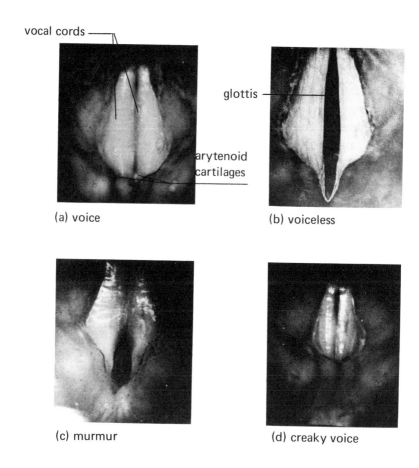

vocal cords

glottis

arytenoid cartilages

(a) voice

(b) voiceless

(c) murmur

(d) creaky voice

Fig. 2. Photographs (by John Ohala and Ralph Vanderslice) of some phonation types. The vocal cords are the white bands running in the vertical direction in each picture. The arytenoid cartilages are clearly visible in the lower part of a and b, and the anterior (ligamental) portions of the vocal cords are in the upper part of each picture.

2. The Phonation Process

In a somewhat speculative article on the phonation process, Catford (1964) describes more than ten states of the vocal cords which are linguistically significant. The evidence for some of these states is a little vague, as Catford himself is well aware; he explicitly states that his article is only a preliminary attempt at setting up a scheme of categories for types of phonation. But most phoneticians would agree that we probably need at least six or seven states of the vocal cords to account for the linguistic oppositions which occur within languages. These states are summarized in table 1, and some of them are illustrated in the photographs (taken by John Ohala and Ralph Vanderslice) in figure 2.

The positions in voiced and voiceless sounds are too well known to need much further comment here (see fig. 2a, b). In the formation of a voiced sound the vocal cords are adjusted so that they are almost touching along their entire length. The result of air flowing through this constriction is a suction effect which draws the vocal cords together. But as soon as they are together there is no flow, and consequently no action pulling them together; so they come apart and release the pressure which has been built up beneath them. But when they are apart they are again subject to the suction caused by the outgoing air. So the cycle repeats itself, producing the regular vibrations known as voice.

The rate of vibration during a voiced sound depends on two factors: the tension of the vocal cords and the pressure drop across them. The pitch will rise whenever either of these two factors is increased, as is explained elsewhere (Ladefoged 1967). The forces exerting tension on the vocal cords can also be divided into two groups: the muscles of the larynx, and the articulatory movements of the tongue which tend to raise the larynx and stretch the vocal cords. Changes in pitch which are linguistically significant are either due to changes in the pressure of the air below the vocal cords or to changes in the tension of the vocal cords caused by the action of the muscles of the larynx; changes due to other movements have been shown to be predictable in all languages so far observed. Thus in a tone language the actual frequency of vibration during the occurrence of a particular tone has been shown to be slightly higher in a syllable containing the vowel i , in which the larynx tends to be pulled upward by the high tongue position, than in a similar syllable containing a more open vowel such as a (Ladefoged 1964a). In an intonation language such as English the frequency of the peak of an intonation contour depends in a similar way on the vowel quality (Lehiste and Peterson 1961). Neither of these variations is linguistically significant.

Table 1 Some states of the glottis

Phonetic term	Brief description	Symbols
Voice	Vibration of the vocal cords	m z b a
Voiceless	Vocal cords apart	m̥ s p h
Aspiration	A brief period of voicelessness during and immediately after the release of an articulatory stricture	s ʰ p ʰ
Murmur	"Breathy voice" — arytenoids apart, ligamental vocal cords vibrating	m̤ z̤ b̤
Laryngealization	"Creaky voice" — arytenoids tightly together, but a small length of the ligamental vocal cords vibrating	m̰ z̰ b̰
Glottal stop	Vocal cords held together	ʔ
Whisper	Vocal cords together or narrowed except between the arytenoids	(no symbol)

The intonation contour in English utterances usually has a high correlation with the tension of the vocal cords (Ladefoged 1963, 1967; Ohala 1970); and in nearly all circumstances laryngeal adjustments of this kind are the major determiners of pitch changes. But it appears (Ladefoged 1968) that the high pitch which occurs at the end of tag questions such as "It's true, isn't it?" may also be associated with an increase in the pressure of the air below the vocal cords in many speakers. More recent studies as yet unpublished indicate that in a tone language such as Yoruba there is often an increase in subglottal pressure during high tones.

During voiceless sounds the vocal cords are apart at the posterior end, between the arytenoid cartilages (see fig. 2b). They are not, however, pulled as far apart as possible. In normal expiration they are slightly closer together than they are in inspiration, and as far as is known the position during voiceless sounds is the same as that during expiration. This difference between inspiration and expiration may be why h sounds are sometimes said to have a slightly narrowed position of the vocal cords; but the position for an h which is not between voiced sounds is probably the same as in any other voiceless sound. In fact, h is often simply a phonologically convenient way of designating a sound which is the voiceless counterpart of the adjacent (usually the following) sound.

Many linguistic contrasts can be characterized simply by means of the oppositions voiced–voiceless, and aspirated–unaspirated (cf. Lisker and Abramson 1964). We shall use all these as technical terms with precise definitions. Voiced and voiceless refer to specific states of the vocal cords occurring during the articulation of a sound. If a sound is said to be partially voiced (or voiceless), the state of the vocal cords is that for voice (or voicelessness) during only part of the articulation. English initial b may be said to be usually partly voiced, whereas French initial b is nearly always fully voiced. Aspirated and unaspirated refer to the state of the vocal cords during and immediately after the release of an articulatory stricture. In any aspirated sound the vocal cords are in the voiceless position during the release; in an unaspirated sound they are in a voiced position during this period. In a voiceless unaspirated sound they start vibrating at about the same time as the stricture is released; and in a voiced sound they vibrate during both the closure and its release. The three possibilities are given in figure 3 (cf. Abercrombie 1967 for a similar diagram). It should be noted that the fourth possibility, a voiced aspirated sound, would, from the standpoint of these definitions, be a sound in which the vocal cords were vibrating during the articulation and then came apart into the voiceless position during the release of the stricture. Such a sound has not yet been observed in any language; we will consider later the structure of sounds such as Hindi bɦ dɦ gɦ , which are often called voiced aspirates.

The definition of aspiration found in American phonetic literature sometimes refers to the release of an extra puff of air. This usage is not really specific enough. There are at least two possibilities as to how this extra puff of

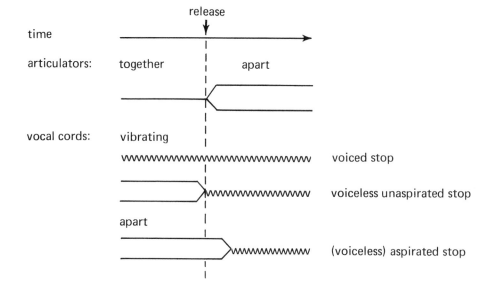

Fig. 3. The relation between the timing of the articulatory movements and the state of the glottis in some stop consonants. Note that the terms voiced—voiceless refer only to the state of the glottis during the articulatory stricture, and the terms aspirated—unaspirated only to the state of the glottis during and immediately after the release of the stricture.

air might be produced: it could be the result of an extra push from the respiratory muscles, or it could be due to a valvelike action of the glottis, allowing more air to be released. If we want our phonetic descriptions to embody a precise account of how a speaker makes a sound we should avoid a usage which permits the specification of two different actions which in fact produce different sounds.

Contrasts between voiced and voiceless versions of nearly all types of sounds occur. Examples of languages having simple contrasts between voiced and voiceless stops and fricatives need not be given here. Voiced and voiceless nasals and laterals occur in a number of languages; examples of contrasts in Burmese are given in table 2. An acoustic analysis of the consonants in the words in the second and fourth lines as said by two informants showed that in each instance voicing began shortly before the closure was released. I do not know if this is typical of all speakers and all languages having contrasts of this kind, but if it is, perhaps these sounds should be called partially voiced as opposed to fully voiced. Voiceless semivowels such as those in Scottish English *which* (as opposed to *witch*) also have the voicing starting before the steady state of the vowel has begun; but it is largely an arbitrary question whether this point should be taken as marking the end of the semivowel. Voiceless vowels occur as allophones in many languages. As a surface phonetic phenomenom they are an important areal feature of the Amerindian languages of the Plains and the Rockies. But, at least in Comanche (Hamp 1958) and Cheyenne (Davis 1962), they are not underlying phonemes. According to Lounsbury (personal communication) none of the cases cited in the literature on Amerindian languages actually constitute examples of phonemic contrasts between voiced and voiceless vowels.

Table 2 Voiced and voiceless nasals and laterals in Burmese. Voiceless segments are indicated by a small open circle under the symbol.

m̀a	healthy	nà	pain	ŋâ	fish
m̥à	order	n̥à	nostril	ŋ̥â	rent
		l a	moon		
		l̥ã	beautiful		

Contrasts between aspirated and unaspirated sounds are common among stop consonants. Many languages have three-way oppositions, as exemplified by the Thai words in table 3. Aspirated and unaspirated fricatives also occur, but three-way contrasts are less common; Burmese examples are given in table 4. As far as I know no language uses a contrast between aspirated and unaspirated semivowels, although it is perfectly easy to distinguish between sequences such as ʍhɑ and ʍɑ . Sounds in which a period of voicelessness occurs before and during the formation of a stricture are said to be preaspirated; unit phonemes of this kind occur in the Gaelic of the Hebrides and Icelandic.

Table 3 Aspirated, voiceless unaspirated, and voiced stops in Thai. Aspirated segments are indicated by a following raised h .

pʰàa	to split	tʰam	to do	kʰàt	to interrupt
pàa	forest	tam	to pound	kàt	to bite
bàa	shoulder	dam	black		

Table 4 Voiced, voiceless unaspirated, and aspirated fricatives in Burmese

zãn	levitation	zauŋ	edge
sãn	example	sauŋ	harp
sʰãn	rice	sʰauŋ	winter

Many sounds cannot be characterized in terms of the two states of the vocal cords, voiced and voiceless. In Gujarati, and in several other Indian languages, there is an apparent opposition in ordinary informal speech between two sets of vowels, in both of which the vocal cords are vibrating. Firth (1957) described one as having tight phonation and the other breathy phonation. I prefer to follow Pandit (1957) in referring to one as voice and the other as murmur. In the one set I can find no difference from the kind of vibrations of the vocal cords described above as voice. The other set is distinguished by a different adjustment of the vocal cords in which the posterior portions (between the arytenoid cartilages) are held apart, while the ligamental parts are allowed to vibrate (see fig. 2c). There is a high rate of flow of air out of the lungs during these sounds; so the term breathy voice is also appropriate. English / h / between vowels (as in *ahead*) has a similar quality.

In Gujarati this third state of the vocal cords, which is quite different from that for voiced or voiceless sounds, may not be accompanied by an extra push of the respiratory muscles; the different mode of vibration of the vocal cords is due to a different adjustment of the larynx. The examples in table 5 show that murmur can occur during both consonants and vowels (or, as Firth might have put it, it can be prosody of either syllable initials or syllable finals). There is no agreed IPA diacritic for marking this kind of phonation. I have used a diaeresis under the symbol. The phonemicization suggested by Pandit (1957) is also shown. But on historical grounds (and because Gujarati does not have a contrast between voiced and murmured vowels after murmured consonants) it

Table 5 Murmured stops and vowels in Gujarati, showing both the phonemicization suggested by Pandit (1957) and a transcription indicating the phonetic segments. Murmured segments are indicated by a diaeresis under the symbol.

/bar/	[baɾ]	twelve	/pɔr/	[pɔɾ]	last year
/bahr/	[ba̤ɾ]	outside	/pɔhr/	[pɔ̤r]	early morning
/bhar/	[ba̤ɾ]	burden	/pʰɔdz/	[pʰɔdz]	army
/aṛ/	[aṛ̥]	obstruction	/ahṛ/	[a̤ṛ̤]	bones

seems probable that this phonemicization does not really reflect the differences between the underlying forms. The words containing murmured vowels could always be said to have an extra syllable in the underlying forms consisting of a vowel plus /h/.

Most Indo-Aryan languages have a series of stops with a murmured release, in addition to a three-way contrast between voiced, voiceless unaspirated, and (voiceless) aspirated stops as described above. In all the languages I have examined (Hindi, Sindhi, Marathi, Bengali, Assamese, Gujarati, Bihari, Marwari, and others) the murmured stops are clearly distinguished by having a different mode of vibration of the vocal cords. There are minor variations (Saurashtri, as spoken at Madurai, sounds as if the release of the stops is accompanied by a brief period of voice before the murmur), but one cannot construct a model which will generate these sounds without allowing for three distinct states of the vocal cords. It was for this reason that the murmured sounds could not be fitted into the scheme of figure 3, which symbolizes only two different states of the vocal cords. There is, it is true, an extra puff of air accompanying both the voiceless aspirated and the murmured stops; but this puff of air is produced in a different way in each case so that the release of the one sounds quite different from the other. Phonemically it may be very convenient to symbolize these sounds as /b bh p ph/, and so on; but when one uses a term such as voiced aspirated, one is using neither the term voiced nor the term aspirated in the same way as in the descriptions of the other stops. Murmured stops could be represented on a diagram like figure 3 only by using a different kind of line to represent a third possible state of the vocal cords.

Murmured consonants occur in a number of languages outside India. They are common in Southern Bantu languages, such as Shona, Tsonga, and members of the Nguni group. In all these languages, during the murmured sounds the vocal cords seem to me to be held slightly closer together than in the Indian languages, so that there is more voice and less breath escaping; nevertheless they contrast clearly with the mode of vibration of the vocal cords which occurs in regular voiced sounds. In Shona there are voiced and murmured nasals. In the Nguni languages Ndebele and Zulu the situation is somewhat similar. There are contrasting voiced and murmured nasals like those in Shona. These sounds, together with a type of h which is realized as a murmured onset of a vowel, and the stops written *b d g* (and perhaps some other consonants) form a phonological class recognizable because they may cause a noticeable lowering of the tone on the subsequent vowel. Phonemically they may be considered to be /mh nh hh bh dh gh/, contrasting at least with /m n h g/. But although the difference between /mh nh/ and /m n/ is that between murmur and voice, and the difference between /hh/ and /h/ is that between murmur and voicelessness, the difference between /gh/ and /g/ seems to be simply that /gh/ is a depressor of the tone on the following vowel; both seem to have ordinary voicing. There are thus two voiced velar stops which are phonemically distinct only because of their influence on the tonal pattern. Ndebele examples are given in table 6.

Table 6 Voiced and murmured nasals, murmured and voiceless approximants (semivowels), and depressor and nondepressor stops in Ndebele (examples and analysis suggested by George Fortune)

/úmúntu/	[úmúntu]	person
/úmhámha/	[úmâma]	my mother
/úgúna/	[úgúna]	to run
/úm̥nháwámi/	[úm̥náwámi]	my young brother
/úgúhámba/	[úgúhámba]	to travel
/úgúhhúla/	[úgúɦûla]	to be a prostitute
/égúvugéni/	[égúvugéni]	on getting up
/égúgughéni/	[égúgugêni]	on growing old

/gh/ = [g which depresses following high tone]

Another mode of vibration of the vocal cords occurs in laryngealized sounds. In this type of phonation the arytenoid cartilages are pressed inward so that the posterior portions of the vocal cords are held together and only the anterior (ligamental) portions are able to vibrate (see fig. 2*d*). The result is often a harsh sound with a comparatively low pitch. It is also known as vocal fry (Moore and von Leden 1958) and creaky voice. Catford (1964) distinguishes between creak and creaky voice, but I am not sure this distinction is needed for a theory of linguistic phonetics.

The opposition between voicing and laryngealization occurs during both semivowels and stops in Chadic languages such as Hausa, Bura, and Margi. Laryngealized phonation is indicated by a subscript tilde in the Margi examples cited in table 7. In these words, as in similar forms in related Chadic languages, laryngealized voicing is often audible in the adjacent vowels; but the laryngealization is regarded as a feature of the consonant not only on the phonetic grounds that it is clearly more evident during the consonant, but also on the distributional grounds that it occurs on all vowels, but only when adjacent to these certain consonants. In Nilotic languages such as Ateso and Lango there is another form of laryngealization which is used to distinguish a set of five vowels from a similar set with more normal voicing. Examples are given in table 8. These languages have significant tones which can occur with either kind of phonation. The auditory difference between the two sets of

Table 7 Contrasts involving laryngealized stops and semivowels in Margi (from Ladefoged 1964a; suggested by Hoffman 1963). Laryngealization is indicated by a tilde under the symbol.

pádó	rain	bábál	open place	bàbàl	hard
pʷa	pour in	bʷál	ball	bʷàbʷà	cooked
ptəl	chief	bdàgó	valley	bdàbdó	chewed
tátá	that one	dàlmà	big ax	dàdàhʊ	bitter
мàмà	boiled	káwà	sorry	wáwʃ	adornment
çà	moon	jà	give birth	jà	thigh

Table 8 Contrasts involving laryngealized vowels in Lango

lee	animal	lee	ax
man	this	man	testicles
kor	chest	kor	hen's nest
tur	break	tur	high ground

vowels is that between a slightly harsher, more reverberant sound and one with a softer voicing, nearer to (but not the same as) murmur. There is no report of a language making use of the distinction between laryngealization and murmur, which may lead us to a different way of looking at the phonation types murmur, voice, and laryngealization in a subsequent section.

A fifth state of the glottis which clearly contrasts with both voice and voicelessness is that during a glottal closure, when the vocal cords are held tightly together throughout their length. From a phonological point of view it is often convenient to consider a glottal stop along with articulatory stops such as p t k . But from a phonetic point of view it has to be considered as a state of the glottis, because of the combinatory restrictions; if there is a glottal closure there cannot simultaneously be voice, or voicelessness, or murmur, or laryngealization. Examples of contrasts involving glottal stops in Tagalog are given in table 9.

Table 9   Contrasts involving glottal stops in Tagalog (suggested by Robert Wilson)

ʔaˑnaj	termite	haˑnaj	row
kaʔoˑn	fetch	kahoˑn	box
baˑtaʔ	child	baˑtah	bathrobe
magʔalis	to remove	magalis	full of sores

The final state of the glottis listed in table 1 is that associated with whisper, in which the vocal cords are narrowed or even together anteriorly, leaving a somewhat wider gap at the other end between the arytenoid cartilages. The cords are held rather stiffly, and sometimes there are considerable additional constrictions just above the glottis. This state is linguistically significant only in situations parallel to those in which voiced sounds may be opposed to voiceless sounds. In Wolof in final position, stops and fricatives contrast with their voiceless counterparts; in nonfinal position this same contrast is manifested by a voiced-voiceless opposition. Whisper is often a prosody associated with the otherwise voiced sounds in final syllables in many languages. Doke (1931) reports that it is common in the Bantu family; and it is equally typical of some forms of French.

Table 1 does not show all the linguistic contrasts which are due to differences in the mode of vibration of the vocal cords. There appear to be two different modes underlying the contrasts between the Javanese and Indonesian sounds written with *p* and *b* in words such as *pipi* 'cheek' and *bibi* 'aunt'. Despite the orthography, these sounds do not differ simply by the one being voiced and the other voiceless. The vocal cords vibrate during the same part of the closure in each case, but there is some difference in laryngeal function which is most noticeable during the release of the stop and the first part of the vowel. Different modes of vibration also occur during the release of Korean stops (cf. Kim 1965).

We can account for these differences without having to add to the list of states of the glottis shown in table 1. Some of those states are really more like points on a continuum, which can be split up into a greater number of categories. Figure 4 illustrates one possible way of considering these categories.

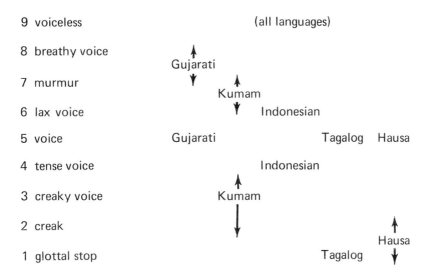

Fig. 4. The feature glottal stricture. As this feature is considered to be a continuum, the numbers and labels attached are arbitrary. No language makes more than three oppositions on this continuum.

It makes the claim (and it should be emphasized that it is only a very tentative claim) that there is a continuum extending from the most closed position, a glottal stop, to the most open position observed in speech, which is that in voiceless sounds. Starting from a glottal stop (which itself may have several degrees of tightness), it is possible to pass through a form of laryngealization (here called creak) in which the arytenoid cartilages are pulled toward one another, and the whole glottis remains constricted except for a small opening in the anterior portion. Slight (but not complete) relaxation of the pulling together of the arytenoids produces the next phonation type, creaky voice, in which a larger proportion of the glottis is vibrating. Then, by further releasing the degree of constriction, one passes through stages which we may call tense voice, voice, and lax voice (though of course recognizing, as with all the stages on this continuum, that there is no predeterminable point at which, for instance, tense voice should be considered to become voice).* Further relaxation leads to a widening of the glottis, particularly between the arytenoids, so that lax voice becomes murmur, in which only the anterior portion is vibrating. This state can arbitrarily be distinguished from one in which there is an even greater rate of flow through the glottis, which we may now call breathy voice. Finally, when even the anterior portion of the glottis is so far apart that it cannot be set in vibration we have the voiceless position.

No language has contrasts involving more than three states and most languages use only two states within this continuum, which we may call that of GLOTTAL STRICTURE. This being so, we can usually, in the classificatory matrices describing phonemes, specify this feature simply in terms of binary possibilities, and then, in the phonological rules leading to the descriptive matrices, rewrite these items in terms of the appropriate values. But in languages such as Kumam, Western Popoloca, and Gujarati, in which the glottal stricture feature can have more than two values, we might use the integers /0 1 2/ in the classificatory matrix; then as a result of a series of context-restricted phonological rules, we may rewrite these values into say, [3 6 9] for some Kumam sounds at the systematic phonetic level, or [5 8 9] for some Gujarati sounds at this level. As was noted before, the particular numbers (and names) used for the different degrees of glottal stricture are the product of an arbitrary assignment within the theory of general phonetics. But once this assignment has been made, the phonological rules for individual languages can generate phones which can be compared not only with each other but also with the phones of other languages.

---

*A recent paper (Halle and Stevens 1971) has suggested the terms stiff (instead of tense) voice, and slack (instead of lax) voice.

There is a great deal of explanatory power in the concept of a feature of glottal stricture on which some of the glottal states are rank ordered. A feature of this kind makes a number of linguistic facts easier to explain. Murmured or breathy voiced sounds are between voiced and voiceless sounds, and hence can be grouped with either of them; this is as it should be for appropriate descriptions of languages such as Shona and Punjabi. Similarly voiced sounds and different forms of laryngealized sounds are a more closely related natural class than laryngealized sounds and voiceless sounds, which is what is required in descriptions of Kumam. Furthermore this formulation assists us in making statements about coarticulated allophones. These allophones, which I formerly called intrinsic allophones (Ladefoged 1965, 1967, 1971a), differ from one another in degree rather than in kind. It is now apparent that, for instance, the allophones of / h / which occur in *that hat* and *my hat* vary in the degree of glottal stricture, and the variations are predictable from the glottal strictures in the adjacent sounds. The alternations between laryngealization and glottal stop which occur in languages such as Sedang (Smith 1968) and Western Popoloca (Williams and Pike 1968) may be explicable in a similar way.

The only major difficulty with this oversimplified description of the states of the glottis is that it leaves no way of accounting for whispered sounds. A number of languages (such as French and Wolof) have contrasts between whispered and voiceless sounds in the environment of pause, which are in complementary distribution with contrasts between voiced and voiceless sounds in other environments. In these circumstances whisper would appear to be a coarticulated allophone of voice. I am not sure of the best way of dealing with this problem, since even these forms of whisper cannot be described simply in terms of the relaxation of the pull between the arytenoids.

The other state of the glottis which has been left out of the discussion in this part of this chapter is that which occurs in aspirated sounds. This state might have been regarded as an extension beyond the voiceless position in the glottal stricture feature, in that it designates sounds in which the minimum degree of glottal stricture is maintained for longer than usual. This point of view has been well developed by Kim (1970), who shows that (at least in Korean stops) there is a good correlation between the duration of aspiration and the extent to which the vocal cords are drawn apart during the stop closure. But it is possible to derive a more appropriate set of natural classes for use in phonological descriptions if it is considered part of a separate feature, to be called VOICE ONSET, which specifies the moment of onset of regular voicing (cf. Lisker and Abramson 1964). This feature is also a continuum along which we may consider a number of values as shown in figure 5 (cf. also fig. 3).

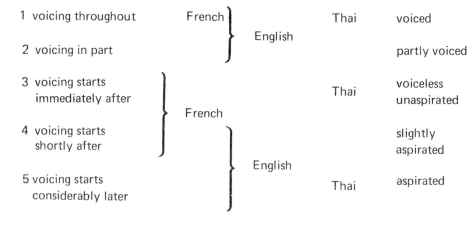

1 voicing throughout	French			Thai	voiced
2 voicing in part		English			partly voiced
3 voicing starts immediately after				Thai	voiceless unaspirated
4 voicing starts shortly after	French				slightly aspirated
5 voicing starts considerably later			English	Thai	aspirated

Fig. 5. The feature voice onset. As this feature is considered to be a continuum the divisions are arbitrary. No language contrasts more than three points on this scale; it applies only to stops and fricatives.

Most languages use only a binary opposition, and no language contrasts more than three possibilities.

At first glance it might seem as if there is a great deal of overlap between the two features dealing with aspects of glottal activity; and it is certainly true that there is some redundancy in specifications using both features, in that, for example, a glottal stop necessarily implies no vibration. But many of the glottal strictures can be regarded as occurring with several of the voice onset possibilities. The independence of the two features is demonstrated by the data shown in figure 6, some of which should be regarded as tentative.

It seems that this kind of analysis differentiates sounds in terms of appropriate natural classes. The Korean stops are arranged as suggested by Kim (1965): there are two sets of stops with tense voicing, which are distinguished from each other by variations within the voice onset feature; and there is a third set which is distinguished from the other two by having lax voicing, but

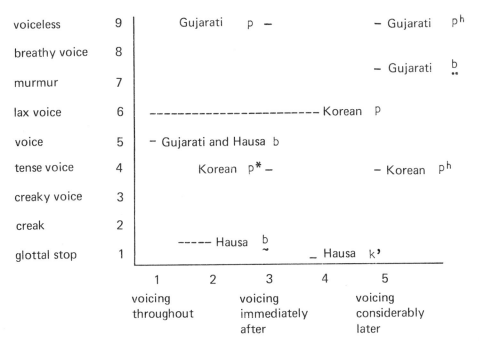

voiceless	9
breathy voice	8
murmur	7
lax voice	6
voice	5
tense voice	4
creaky voice	3
creak	2
glottal stop	1

Gujarati p —   — Gujarati p^h

— Gujarati b̤

———————————— Korean p

— Gujarati and Hausa b

Korean p* —   — Korean p^h

————— Hausa b̰   ＿ Hausa k'

1	2	3	4	5
voicing throughout		voicing immediately after		voicing considerably later

Fig. 6. A (tentative) arrangement of some stop consonants, showing the relation between the two features dealing with aspects of glottal activity.

for which the voice onset feature is contextually determined, since the allophones may vary from being fully voiced to being slightly aspirated. Among the Gujarati stops, the maximum differentiation is between b and p h ; the two sounds b̤ and p h are alike in their voice onset time; p and p h are alike in their degree of glottal stricture.

A suggestion is also made in this figure concerning the categorization of some of the Hausa stops. This language contains a set of voiced stops, a set of voiceless stops, and a set of glottalized stops which includes the laryngealized sounds b̰ and d̰ and the ejective k '. The latter sound (like other ejectives, which will be discussed in the next chapter) can be said to have a glottal closure (state 1) throughout the articulation and for a short period after its release, before the beginning of regular voicing. It thus appears on the chart very close to b̰ and d̰. At the systematic phonemic level all these sounds may be said to have the maximum degree of glottal stricture and may be marked /1/, Hausa having the possibilities /1 2 3/ for the feature at this level. Through the application of the phonological rules they would come to have the systematic phonetic values indicates in figure 6.

Hausa can be handled within the Jakobsonian framework by the use of the feature checked (glottalized)–unchecked. But it is often impossible to achieve correct natural classes in other languages by means of binary specifications such as voiced–voiceless, aspirated–unaspirated, or fortis–lenis. This is especially true if we require our features to define real properties and not to be merely names summarizing disparate phenomena occurring in different circumstances.

3. The Airstream Process

The principal airstream mechanisms are summarized in table 10. Nearly all speech is formed with a pulmonic egressive airstream, in which air is pushed out of the lungs mainly under the control of the internal intercostal muscles. The physiological mechanisms involved in producing this airstream are discussed in some detail in Ladefoged (1967). Some communities use an ingressive pulmonic airstream for paralinguistic purposes, such as disguising the voice (Conklin 1949). But I have not heard of any language making a linguistic contrast by using an ingressive as opposed to an egressive pulmonic airstream. It would probably be too inconvenient (if not impossible) to reverse the action of the respiratory mechanism with sufficient dexterity.

Table 10 The principal airstream mechanisms

Airstream	Direction	Brief description	Type of stop	Symbols
Pulmonic	Egressive	Lung air pushed out under the control of the respiratory muscles	Plosive	p t k
Glottalic	Egressive	Pharynx air compressed by the upward movement of the closed glottis	Ejective	pʼ tʼ kʼ
Glottalic	Ingressive	Downward movement of the vibrating glottis	Implosive	ɓ ɗ ɠ
Velaric	Ingressive	Mouth air rarefied by the backward and downward movement of the tongue	Click	ǀ ʗ ʖ

Variations in the way the pulmonic egressive airstream is produced can be correlated with increases in subglottal pressure which produce significant variations in pitch (as discussed above). Increases in subglottal pressure can also be correlated with variations in stress. Phonetic literature is full of vague remarks about the nature of stress; but the data summarized in Ladefoged (1967) show conclusively that a primary or secondary stress involves a gesture of the respiratory muscles which can be quantified in terms of the amount of work done on the air in the lungs. Recent work (Netsell 1970; Ohala 1970) indicates that variations in stress may be also accompanied by laryngeal adjustments.

Variations in the degree of activity of the respiratory muscles may be responsible for some of the differences between fortis and lenis sounds. I doubt whether such variations actually occur during most of the sounds which have been described as being fortis as opposed to lenis. Lisker and Abramson (1964) are probably correct in saying that nearly all these sounds vary only in the relations between the time at which voicing commences and the time at which the stricture is released; consequently these sounds can be specified adequately by means of terms such as voiced, voiceless, aspirated, and unaspirated. But there are a few cases which cannot be explained in this way. Pressure recordings indicate that the so-called strong consonants in Luganda are not only usually longer but also pronounced with greater pulmonic pressure than their weak counterparts; examples are given in table 11. The so-called fortis stops in Korean (examples in table 12; cf. Kim 1965) may also be associated with greater action of the respiratory muscles, but in this language there are additional differences in the phonation process which are not present in Luganda. There are similar additional complications in the Sino-Tibetan language Kachin-Jingpho, but instrumental recordings show that the so-called fortis nasals in this language are accompanied by a large increase in subglottal

Table 11 Contrasts involving "strong" (or "double") consonants in Luganda. These fortis stops are here transcribed with [*].

páálá	run about madly	ˈp*áápáálʼ	pawpaw
tééká	put	ˈt*éékâ	rule, law
kúlà	grow up	ˈk*úlà	treasure

Table 12 Contrasts involving lenis unaspirated stops, fortis unaspirated stops, and aspirated stops in Korean (suggested by Chin-Wu Kim; cf. Kim 1965). The fortis stops are here transcribed with [*].

pul	fire	p*ul	horn	pʰul	grass
tal	moon, month	t*al	daughter	tʰal	mask
kətta	to walk	k*ətta	extinguished	kʰətta	grew

pressure. Hamp (personal communication) suggests that a similar mechanism may be used for the strong nasals in Albanian.

Although the activity of the respiratory muscles can be varied in degree, the pulmonic egressive airstream mechanism cannot be turned on and off very rapidly. Consequently all sounds in all languages are produced while the air in the lungs is at above atmospheric pressure.

In many languages supplementary airstream mechanisms are involved in the production of speech. Movements of the vocal cords are used in the glottalic airstream mechanism to produce the air pressure variations in the two types of glottalic sounds, ejectives and implosives. An excellent survey of the use of these sounds in many different languages has recently been made by Greenberg (1970).

Ejectives are formed by bringing the vocal cords tightly together and then raising and constricting the whole larynx, so that the pressure of the air in the mouth and pharynx tends to be raised. Contrasting series of stop consonants are made in this way in many African, Amerindian, Caucasian, and other languages, some of which also have ejective fricatives. Examples of both stops and fricatives in Amharic are given in table 13.

Table 13 Contrasts involving ejective stops and fricatives in Amharic. An ejective airstream mechanism is shown by a following apostrophe.

t'ɨl	quarrel	tɨl	warm	dɨl	victory
k'ɨr	stay away	kɨrr	thread	gərr	innocent
mətʃ'	one who comes	mətʃ	when	mədʒ	grinding stone
s'əggɑ	grace	səggɑ	to worry	zəggɑ	to close

It is perfectly possible to produce ingressive glottalic sounds by a similar process in which the closed glottis is rapidly lowered instead of raised. Stops using this mechanism have been reported in Amerindian languages, such as Tojolabal (Pike 1963) and elsewhere. But this type of sound is rare. The more common airstream process involving the lowering of the glottis does not have the vocal cords held tightly together. Instead, as they descend they are allowed to be set in vibration by the air in the lungs, which is always at a higher than atmospheric pressure during any speech activity. The action of the vocal cords in the production of these implosive sounds has been described as that of a leaky piston. Often the piston is so leaky that the airstream is not actually ingressive nor the sounds really implosive. In many of the languages I have observed (cf. Ladefoged 1964a) the pressure of the air in the mouth during an ingressive glottalic stop is approximately the same as that outside the mouth, since the rarefying action of the downward movement of the glottis is almost exactly counterbalanced by the leakage of lung air up through the vocal cords. Although these sounds may be called implosive, in ordinary conversational utterances air seldom flows into the mouth when the stop closure is released.

Some languages which have implosives also have a number of different phonation types. Sindhi has a series of implosive stops in addition to voiced, voiceless unaspirated, aspirated, and murmured stops, so that there are twenty-four contrasting stops in an almost complete five-by-five array, as shown in table 14. (The situation is complicated by the fact that the so-called palatal plosives are actually prepalatal affricates; but the voiced implosive is a true palatal stop.)

Some languages, such as Swahili and Marwari, have implosives as free variants or allophones of voiced pulmonic stops (or plosives). The difference

Table 14 Contrasting stops in Sindhi.

			*	
ɓəni		kʰaɗo	bəɟu	səɠi
curse		pit	run	braid tail
bənu	dəru	gəɗo	ɟəɟu	bəgi
forest	door	dull	judge	buggy
pənu	təru	kʰəʈo	bəcu	ʃəki
leaf	bottom	sour	be safe	suspicious
pʰəɳu	tʰəru	kaʈʰo	bəcʰu	səkʰi
snake hood	district name	assembled	attack	girl friend
bənənu	dəru	kəɗo	vəɟu	səgi
lamentation	trunk of body	take out	opportunity	healthy

* ɟ and c are affricates, and might be transcribed d̠ʐ and t̠ɕ .

26

between implosives and plosives is one of degree rather than of kind. In the formation of voiced plosives in many languages (e.g., English; cf. Hudgins and Stetson 1935) there is often a small downward movement of the vibrating vocal cords. This allows a greater amount of air to pass up through the glottis before the pressure of the air in the mouth has increased so much that there is insufficient difference in pressure from below to above the vocal cords to cause them to vibrate. An implosive is simply a sound in which this downward movement is comparatively large and rapid.

Many of the languages which have ejectives also have implosives, but usually at different points of articulation. Most of the languages which do have both ejectives and implosives at the same place of articulation seem to lack one or other of the corresponding pulmonic voiced and voiceless stops. Thus Maidu (Shipley 1953, 1964) has p' ɓ p , but no b , and t' ɗ t , but no d . Some of the Nguni languages also have both ejectives and implosive alternants of regular plosives. This tendency for languages to avoid having both ejectives and implosives (other than those which are alternants of plosives) at the same place of articulation has led some investigators (Jakobson 1962; Jakobson and Halle 1956) to consider this mutual exclusion to be a language universal. But recent fieldwork in the Sudan has shown that Uduk has not only ɓ and p' , but also b p pʰ , and a similar alveolar series. Examples are given in table 15.

Table 15 Contrasts involving ejectives and implosives at the same place of articulation in Uduk (a Nilo-Saharan language; examples suggested by Robin Thelwall)

pál	to try	tèr	to collect
pʰálal	centipede	tʰèr	to pour off
p'àchàɗ	fermented	t'èɗ	to lick
ɓà?	back of neck	ɗekʼ	to lift
ba?	to be something	déɗ	to shiver

There are a number of other cases in which the categories we have been defining are not completely discrete. Downward movements of the larynx in some languages are often accompanied by a tendency toward laryngealization. These sounds are in some senses both implosives and laryngealized stops; and in fact no language uses the difference between these two possibilities. There are also no recorded cases of a language using a contrast between an ejective and a plosive preceded by a glottal stop. (But some languages, such as Huixteco Tzotzil, have contrasts between an ejective affricate and an affricate followed by a glottal stop.)

There are other difficulties in that the categories we have outlined so far may need extending to cope with phenomena that have been observed in some languages. I am not altogether certain about the Kachin-Jingpho nasals which were mentioned earlier, partly because there seems to be a parallel phenomenon in the voiceless stops. Kachin-Jingpho has three séries of stops – one which is clearly voiced, one which is clearly voiceless and aspirated, and one, auditorily between the other two, which is largely voiceless and rather unaspirated in which the vocal cords start vibrating and the glottis starts descending shortly before the release of the closure. We may need a feature which will specify what is in common between the (voiced) nasals and the (largely voiceless) stops. It is possible that all these sounds are pronounced with both an increased subglottal pressure and an increase in the glottal stricture, but my data are not completely clear in this regard.

It is perhaps worth noting that the term glottalized has been avoided in all the preceding discussion, largely because it has been used by others in so many different ways. It might be appropriate as a phonological cover term for ejectives, implosives, laryngealized sounds, and pulmonic articulations accompanied by glottal stops. But it is not very useful in precise phonetic descriptions.

There is still another airstream mechanism which we have not yet discussed. This is the velaric airstream mechanism in which a body of air is enclosed by raising the back of the tongue to make contact with the soft palate, and either closing the lips or (more commonly) forming a closure on the teeth or alveolar ridge with the tip (or blade) and sides of the tongue. The air in this chamber is rarefied by the downward and backward movement of the body of the tongue, the back of the tongue maintaining contact with the soft palate. When a more forward part of the closure is released, air rushes into the mouth, and a sound known as a click is produced. This mechanism is always ingressive, and there are no reports of its use in the formation of sounds other than stops; but in some cases plain stops are contrasted with affricates.

The Khoisan languages (e.g., Bushman and Hottentot) and some of the neighboring Southern Bantu languages such as Xhosa and Zulu are the only groups using a velaric airstream mechanism to produce sounds made at a number of different places of articulation. But the air in the mouth is sometimes rarefied in a similar way during the production of labial velar stops in West African languages (cf. Ladefoged 1964a). Zulu and Xhosa have three sets of clicks: dental, alveolar lateral, and postalveolar; the first two often have a slightly affricated quality. The Khoisan languages have clicks at other places of articulation. Lanham (1964) says that the different languages in this group commonly use four out of the six possibilities: bilabial, dental, alveolar, alveolar lateral, palatal, and retroflex. No one language is reported to have more than five of them. Beach (1938), in his description of Hottentot, implies that in some of the clicks in this language there is what we would now call a simultaneous glottalic airstream mechanism. Speakers of the Khoisan languages are no longer readily available, and I have not been able to hear any of them myself.

Since the velaric airstream mechanism involves only movement of mouth air and a velar closure, the pulmonic airstream can be used to produce a velar plosive or a velar nasal which may be formed at the same time as the click, and released slightly later. In addition it is possible for any of the different phonation types to be used. Zulu (like other Nguni languages) has voiced, voiceless unaspirated, and aspirated clicks (velaric sounds accompanied by g , k , and kʰ); and voiced nasal and murmured nasal clicks (velaric sounds accompanied by ŋ and ŋ̈) as shown in table 16. These clicks parallel contrasts between other sounds in language; Zulu also has three-way contrasts among pulmonic stops, and a two-way contrast between voiced and murmured nasals.

When it comes to specifying the differences we have been considering in this chapter in terms of phonetic features, it is appropriate to take into account the combinations that can occur. We do not need to have separate features for each of the four possible airstream mechanisms: pulmonic egressive (plosives), glottalic egressive (ejectives), glottalic ingressive (implosives), and velaric ingressive (clicks).

A pulmonic egressive mechanism occurs in all sounds. For the majority of languages the degree of activity of the respiratory system is a redundant feature at the segmental level, and is contrastive (if at all) only in the formation of different levels of stress (a matter which will be discussed in chapter 9). But, as we have seen, in a small number of languages differences in the degree of activity of the respiratory system characterize strong (fortis) as opposed to weak (lenis) consonants. We will therefore need a feature FORTIS—LENIS, which will be defined as the variations of subglottal pressure which are significant at the segmental level. Since variations in the state of the glottis often occur in conjunction with this feature, it is possible that future research may lead to its definition in a way which takes the laryngeal activity into account.

Table 16 Contrasting clicks in Zulu. All these items are imperative forms of verbs, all with the tone pattern low-high (examples suggested by L.W. Lanham)

	(Laminal) dental	(Apical) postalveolar	Alveolar lateral
Aspirated	ǀʰaǀʰa be evident	ǃʰaǃʰa rip open	ʖʰoʖʰa stab, jab
Voiceless unaspirated	ǀaǀa climb	ǃaǃa explain	ʖoʖa narrate
Voiced	g͡ǀag͡ǀa dance at wedding	g͡ǃoka dress up	g͡ʖoba pound
Voiced nasal	ŋ͡ǀoŋ͡ǀa gather unripe corn	ŋ͡ǃala tie tightly	ŋ͡ʖaŋ͡ʖa coax
Murmured nasal	ŋ͡ǀäŋ͡ǀa act quickly	ŋ͡ǃoŋ͡ǃa resound	ŋ͡ʖola slope

In addition, we must set up two other features concerned with airstream mechanisms. The first, which we will call GLOTTALICNESS, uses the fact that implosives and ejectives differ in terms of the single parameter of rate of vertical laryngeal movement toward the lungs. At the systematic phonetic level, ejectives would then be specified by a negative number, and implosives by a positive number, the magnitude of the number indicating the degree of force with which the glottalic airstream mechanism was used. Such a specification provides a nice way of describing weakly implosive allophones which occur in many languages in certain environments; and it also formalizes the fact that a sound cannot be simultaneously an ejective and an implosive. We may consider the zero degree of this feature to be that which occurs in ordinary pulmonic sounds in which there is no movement of the larynx. As we have noted, it is extremely unusual for a language to contrast three degrees of this feature by having, at one place of articulation, implosives, plosives, and ejectives.

The presence or absence of a velaric airstream mechanism (or, at the systematic phonetic level, the degree of presence of the mechanism) has to be specified separately, by means of a feature we may term VELARIC SUCTION. This permits the possibility of clicks and implosives co-occurring; and it also allows us to give a correct phonetic description of the difference between the powerful clicks in Nguni languages, and the wide range of weak uses of the velaric airstream mechanism which occur in labial velars in West African languages.

It should be noted that all the features which have been proposed so far (glottal stricture and voice onset in the previous chapter, and fortis—lenis, glottalicness, and velaric suction in this chapter) are all continuous scales along which speech sounds may vary. As we have seen, the degree of presence of each of these features is often linguistically significant. For none of these features are there universal phonetic interpretation conventions which specify how the positive occurrence of the feature is to be manifested. Thus, for example, velaric suction is present in some stops in both Idoma of West Africa and Xhosa of South Africa; but the degree to which it is present is very different in the two cases, and is a linguistically significant characteristic of each of these languages.

In subsequent chapters we will find that we cannot always enforce the constraint that sounds differing in terms of a feature should differ only in degree, and that the differences should be quantifiable in terms of a single measurable parameter, as required in Ladefoged (1971a). Moreover it is quite clear that the features discussed so far are not independent variables, which was another requirement of Ladefoged (1971a). We have already noted the constraints on the co-occurrence of some of the values of the glottal stricture and the voice onset features. It also seems as if there is some interaction between these two features and the feature of glottalicness. In a large number of languages (many Bantu languages, many dialects of Hindi), there is a close connection (perhaps free variation) between fully voiced sounds (voice onset 1) and voiced implosives. When we take this in conjunction with the necessity of having a natural class of the kind described for Hausa in figure 6, and the fact that in many languages (including some forms of Hausa) there is free variation between laryngealized stops and implosives, it seems apparent that we must regard sounds with a glottalic airstream mechanism as being specified in terms of a feature which interacts with the other two features which are concerned with the state of the glottis in such a way that the values for glottalic sounds can be represented near the appropriate regions of figure 6.

31

4.   The Oro-nasal Process

The oro-nasal process is the simplest of the four major components of the speech mechanism. The soft palate, or velum, may be raised, forming a velic closure in the upper pharnyx; or it may be lowered, allowing air to pass out through the nose. These two possibilities may be distinguished by calling the accompanying sounds either oral or nasal. A common practice, however, is to use the term nasal for a sound in which the oral passage is blocked and all the air passes out through the nose, and the term nasalized for a sound in which the velum is lowered but there is no oral stop closure, so that some of the air passes out through the nose and some through the mouth. This obviates the necessity of calling sounds such as m n nasal stops, and sounds such as b d oral stops.

Many languages distinguish between oral vowels and nasalized vowels. Nasalization of other sounds, such as semivowels, fricatives, and laterals is also common, but in all the languages I have investigated these sounds occur only where one of the adjacent vowels is also nasalized; I do not know of any contrasts between nasalized and nonnasalized semivowels in which an adjacent vowel is not similarly specified by the oro-nasal process. This is, of course, another way of saying that the oro-nasal process often affects a syllable as a whole. Examples of Yoruba contrasts of this kind are given in table 17.

Table 17 Contrasts between oral and nasalized vowels, and examples of (allophonically) nasalized semivowels and other approximants in Yoruba (cf. Ladefoged 1964a). Nasalization is indicated by a superscript tilde.

f í	use	i j a f ĩ	wife	í j ɛ̃	that
ɔ́ b ɔ	monkey	í b ɔ̃	gun	w̃ ɔ́	they
s u	scatter seed	s ũ	push	m ɛ́ r̃ ĩ	four

Another use of the oro-nasal process common in African languages is in the formation of a series of voiced stops which contrast with other fully voiced stops by having a short nasal section during the first part of the articulation. Tiv examples are given in table 18.

There are probably no languages in which it is clearly necessary to recognize two degrees of velic opening in the underlying forms. It is true that

Table 18 Contrasts involving prenasalized stops in Tiv (suggested by David Arnott; cf. Ladefoged 1964*a*).

áa mbὲ	á bὲndὲ	á mὲnà
she suckled	he touched	he swallowed
á ndὲrà	á dὲ	á nὲndà
he began	he left alone	he is backward in growth
á ndzùùr	á dzὲndà	
he muddled	he prohibited	
á ndʒɔyɔi	á dʒîngὲ	á ɲàndὲ
he spoke quickly	he searched	he urinated
á ŋgɔhɔr	á gὲmà	
he received	he turned round	
á ŋm͡gbahom	á g͡bὲɾ	
he approached	he slashed	

there are often allophonic variations: vowels are nasalized to a greater or lesser extent in accordance with the nature of the adjacent consonants; and there is usually a variation in the degree of velic opening in accordance with the height of the vowel (high vowels are far less nasalized than low vowels). But these variations are all easily explicable in terms of the actions of the muscles involved. In fact Moll and Shriner (1967) have shown that nearly all the well-known variations in the degree of velic opening in English (and probably in other languages) can be predicted from a simple model which takes into account only the accompanying articulatory gestures and an on or off instruction to the muscles responsible for the velopharyngeal closure.

In Chinantec (Merrifield 1963) there are clear contrasts between oral, lightly nasalized, and heavily nasalized vowels, as is shown in table 19. These contrasts in the phonetic forms have been instrumentally verified (by William

Table 19 Contrasts involving oral, lightly nasalized, and heavily nasalized vowels in Chinantec (suggested by William Merrifield; cf. Merrifield 1963). In each case the tone is a high to mid glide.

hɑ   so, such   hɑ̃   (he) spreads open   hɑ̃̃   foam, froth

Wang and myself). I do not know if it is necessary to assign an in-between value at the systematic phonemic level. It is possible that the underlying forms differ in the number of segments involved, so that the three-way contrasts between oral, lightly nasalized, and heavily nasalized vowels are really contrasts of the form a – ã – ãn or a – an – ãn , the final consonants not appearing in the phonetic output.

The categorization of sounds involving the oro-nasal process is comparatively simple. There is the possibility of having three basic categories: nasal (all the airstream going out through the nose), nasalized (part going out through the nose and part through the mouth), and oral (no air going out through the nose). But this is an unmotivated complication in comparison with a simple feature which we will call NASALITY, which is defined in terms of the degree of velopharyngeal closure. In the vast majority of languages, at the systematic phonemic level only two degrees need be assigned: if the soft palate is raised so that there is virtually complete closure, the sound may be said to have a value of /0/ on this parameter (i.e., to be oral); if it is not it will have a value of /1/ (and be called nasal). In a language such as Chinantec it may be necessary to assign intermediate values even at the systematic phonemic level, but this is by no means clear at the moment.

An additional feature, PRENASALITY, is also necessary. This feature, like the voice onset feature considered in a previous chapter, must be defined in terms of the duration of an event. It is the duration of the velopharyngeal opening which occurs before another articulation such as an oral stop or fricative in circumstances which require the whole complex to be considered as one phonological unit. Only the values 0 or 1 are possible for this feature at the systematic phonemic level; but languages probably differ in the values they use at the systematic phonetic level.

35

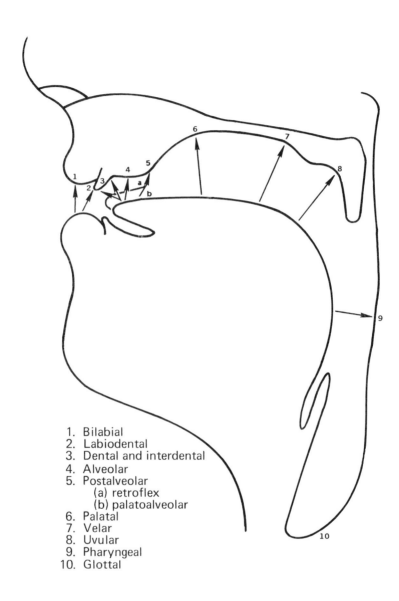

1. Bilabial
2. Labiodental
3. Dental and interdental
4. Alveolar
5. Postalveolar
    (a) retroflex
    (b) palatoalveolar
6. Palatal
7. Velar
8. Uvular
9. Pharyngeal
10. Glottal

Fig. 7. A preliminary list of some places of articulation.

5.   Places Of Articulation

One of the difficulties of talking about places of articulation is that neither the tongue nor the roof of the mouth can be divided into discrete sections. The teeth are arranged on the alveolar ridge in such a way that it is difficult to divide dental from alveolar. The extent of the alveolar region is also indeterminate. The end of the alveolar ridge has been defined by Jones (1956) as the point where the roof of the mouth ceases being concave and becomes convex, but when one looks at actual data on mouth shapes it is often difficult or impossible to locate this point; in any case it makes the center of the alveolar region much farther back than in the articulations phoneticians commonly call alveolar. The diagrams of English alveolar t in Jones's works show an articulation more retracted than that made by any English speaker I have investigated. The center of the palatal region is equally hard to define, although here Jones has a more useful concept in his use (e.g., in Jones 1956, and in International Phonetic Association 1949) of the term cardinal palatal to mean (apparently; I cannot find an explicit definition to this effect) an articulation in the area of cardinal vowel number one (the highest and most front vowel possible). The category velar can be defined by relation to the soft palate as opposed to the hard, but this division is also difficult to locate in practice. And the distinction between velar and uvular is even more arbitrary. In fact, when discussing places of articulation it seems especially necessary to bear in mind that the categories are required simply for distinguishing linguistic oppositions.

A preliminary set of categories of place of articulation is represented diagrammatically in figure 7. Each of the terms defines an action of both a lower and an upper articulator. There is little difficulty about the first two terms. Bilabial stops and nasals occur in nearly all languages. Some languages also have bilabial fricatives which have to be distinguished from labiodental fricatives; examples from Ewe, which contracts both voiced and voiceless sounds of this kind, are shown in table 20. From my own work I know of contrasts between bilabials and labiodentals only among fricatives and what we shall call approximants (frictionless continuants and semivowels). Labiodental nasals occur in many languages, but probably only as coarticulated allophones of other nasals. Labiodental stops contrasting with bilabial stops have been reported in Tonga (Guthrie 1948), but I did not succeed in eliciting them from my Tonga informants. I have, however, heard a labiodental stop made by a Shubi speaker with good teeth. For this speaker this sound was clearly in contrast with a bilabial stop; but I suspect that the majority of Shubi speakers

Table 20 Contrasts involving bilabial and labiodental fricatives in Ewe (suggested by Gilbert Ansre; cf. Ladefoged 1964a)

Bilabials		Labiodentals	
ɛβɛ̀	the Ewe language	ɛ̀vɛ̀	two
éɸá	he polished	éfá	he was cold
àβló	mushroom	évló	he is evil
éɸlè	he bought	éflě	he split off

make the contrast one of labial stop versus affricate, rather than bilabial versus labiodental stop. Another somewhat anomalous sound which I have not heard myself is a linguolabial stop, in which the tongue makes contact with the upper lip; this sound is mentioned by Hockett (1955) as occurring in Bororo, but I gather from Lounsbury (personal communication) that the reference should really have been to another South American language, Umotina.

It may be necessary to distinguish between dentals and interdentals, but I do not know of any use of this distinction. However the categories dental, alveolar, and postalveolar undoubtedly need further differentiation. Sounds in each of these three categories can be made with either the tongue tip (in which case they are called apical) or the tongue blade (in which case they are laminal). There are thus six possible combinations; but no language uses more than three of them. Some of the Dravidian languages, such as Malayalam, have three stops and three nasals in this region, all of them being made with the tip of the tongue. The Dravidian languages seem to be the only ones in which contrasts involving these nearby places of articulation on the roof of the mouth do not also involve a different part of the tongue. Among West African languages the contrasts are between apical dentals and laminal alveolars, or between apical alveolars and laminal dentals (in which the tongue contact usually extends beyond the teeth, so that they are really dentialveolars). Table 21 lists some languages using these sounds, together with exemplifying symbols and a possible terminology which can be used if it is thought desirable to incorporate the apical–laminal distinction into the set of terms applying to place of articulation. The examples given in table 21 have been illustrated by instrumental data and discussed in detail elsewhere (Ladefoged 1964a). Contrasts involving stops and nasals in Malayalam are illustrated in table 22; the bilabial,

Table 21 Symbols and terminology for dental and alveolar articulations, and examples from West African languages; the laminal articulations are usually affricated (cf. Ladefoged 1964*a*). The alternative specifications in the last column are discussed in the text.

	tip	tip + blade	tip	blade	tip	blade
Lower articulator	tip	tip + blade	tip	blade	tip	blade
Upper articulator	teeth	teeth + ridge	front of teeth ridge		back of teeth ridge	
Features	apical	laminal dental	apical	laminal alveolar	apical	laminal postalveolar
Label summarizing articulators	dental	dentialveolar	apical alveolar	laminal alveolar	retroflex	palato-alveolar
Example of symbol	d̪	d̪	d	d̬	ḍ	d̲ or ɟ
Exemplifying language						
Temne	t̪ or descend			t̬ or farms		
Isoko	òtú louse		òtú gang			
Ewe	édà he throws				édà she laid	
Twi			ɔ́dà he lies			àdá (or) àɟá father

palatal, and velar nasal articulations are also exemplified, so that it may be plainly seen that this language has six contrasting places of articulation.

Basque is reported to have a contrast between an apical and a laminal s , but I do not know if both sounds have the same place of articulation. None of the languages that I have heard myself uses a contrast between an apical and a laminal articulation at the same place. Although we clearly need the three places of articulation, dental, alveolar, and postalveolar as shown in table 22, we may not need, at the systematic phonemic level, the subdivisions of each of these places as shown in table 21. The apical–laminal distinctions could be said to function simply as intensifiers of the small differences in the place of articulation. However, as we shall see when we come to discuss manners of articulation, the apical–laminal distinction may be needed when we consider all the fricatives that can occur.

Both retroflex (i.e., apical postalveolar) sounds and palatoalveolar (i.e., laminal postalveolar) sounds cover a wide range of articulatory areas. In some South Asian languages the retroflex consonants involve only the tip of the

Table 22

Table 22 Contrasts involving bilabial, dental, alveolar, postalveolar, palatal, and velar places of articulation in Malayalam, illustrating the necessity for six points of articulation. Dental articulations are indicated by a subscript of the form $_{\_}$. Retroflex articulations are indicated by a subscript dot.

Bilabial	Dental	Alveolar	Postalveolar	Palatal	Velar
	mut̪t̪u	muttu	muṭṭu		
	pearl	density	knee		
	kut̪t̪i	kutti	kuṭṭi		
	stabbed	peg	child		
kʌmmi	pʌn̪n̪i	kʌnni	kʌṇṇi	kʌɲɲi	kʌŋŋi
shortage	pig	Virgo	link in chain	boiled rice and water	crushed
en̪n̪ʌ	enne	eṇṇʌ	teːɲɲʌ	teːŋŋʌ	
named	me	oil	worn out	coconut	

tongue and the back of the alveolar ridge, whereas in others there is contact between a large part of the underside of the tongue tip and much of the forward part of the hard palate. Similarly the actual area of contact in palatoalveolars may vary over a wide range, so that it is often hard to decide whether a given sound should be classified as a palatoalveolar or a palatal. In fact, it seems probable that no language distinguishes between sounds simply by one being a palatal and the other a palatoalveolar. All the languages which use these two articulatory positions (such as Ngwo, illustrated by palatograms in Ladefoged 1964a) either have affricates in the one position and stops in the other, or in some other way supplement the contrasts in place of articulation with additional variations in the manner of articulation. We may have no justification for attempting to distinguish between these two categories. It was for this reason that alternative symbols were given in the last column of table 22.

Contrasts between palatals, velars, and uvulars are illustrated in table 23, which lists plosive and ejective examples from Quechua. The palatal stops in many languages tend to be more affricated than the others, perhaps because of the mechanical difficulty of quickly withdrawing the front of the tongue, which often contacts a large area of the roof of the mouth in the formation of these stops. I do not know of any language which distinguishes between a palatal stop and either a palatal affricate or the sequence palatal stop followed by palatal fricative.

Table 23 Contrasts involving palatal, velar, and uvular stops in Quechua (suggested by Peter Landerman). The palatal stops are strongly affricated.

Palatal	c i r i	cold	c^h i l c i	drizzle	c , i c i	dirty
Velar	k i r u	tooth	k^h i p u	Kipu	k , i c i j	pinch
Uvular	q a r a	skin	q^h a p a n	rich	q , a c u	grass

Stops, nasals, and fricatives occur at all the places of articulation discussed so far, with the exception of the labiodental category. The illustrations given have been mainly of stops and nasals; fricatives and other manners of articulation such as laterals and trills will be considered later. In the pharyngeal area, however, no language uses stops (most people cannot make them), and nasals are an impossibility. Even fricatives are not very common. Table 24 gives examples (suggested by Ferguson et al. 1961) of pharyngeal fricatives in Arabic and some auditorily similar sounds with different phonation types. These contrasts (and similar examples in other languages) are additionally interesting in that they suggest that we should consider some sounds which are characterized by particular kinds of activity in the larynx as having not only a particular phonation type but also a glottal place of articulation. The alternation of a glottal stop with other stops as part of a regular series of stops also strongly suggests that we should consider the glottis as a possible place of articulation. (This dual role of the glottis in phonetic taxonomies has been well described by Catford 1968.)

So far we have been considering only consonants in this survey of possible places of articulation; and, as we shall see in chapter 8, where we discuss the

Table 24 Contrasts involving laryngealized and voiceless pharyngeal approximants or fricatives, murmured approximants, and glottal stops in Arabic (Cf. Ferguson et al. 1961)

Laryngealized pharyngeals	ʕa l a	ʕamm	waaʕʕa
	on	paternal uncle	container
Voiceless pharyngeals	ħa l l a?	ħamm	
	right away	concern	
Murmured approximants	ɦa l a?	ɦammaam	waaɦed
	shave	bath	one
Glottal stops	?aḷḷa	?amar	wa??af
	God	command	stop

specification of vowels in detail, the set of features which is required for characterizing vowels is largely different from the set required for consonants. But there are good reasons for considering all sounds, including both vowels and consonants, in terms of the same set of places of articulation. By doing this we can give an explanatory account of many phenomena involving assimilations. The phonological descriptions of languages frequently require statements showing how s is realized as ʃ in the environment of high front vowels, and how vowels become diphthongs with a w offglide in the environment of velar consonants. We could, of course, simply make statements of this kind and not go any further. But if we did only this we would not be saying very much about how languages work. Our descriptions would contain equally complex statements for s becoming ʃ in the environment of i as they would for s becoming ʃ in the environment of o , although these are clearly not equally complex phenomena. We can write rules which have much more explanatory power if we consider vowels such as i to be similar to postalveolar (palatoalveolar) sounds, u to be similar to velar sounds, and perhaps o and ɑ to be in the uvular and pharyngeal regions respectively (cf. Peterson and Shoup 1966).

Bearing this in mind, we may say that there is a feature ARTICULATORY PLACE which we may designate in terms of ten phonetic categories:

(1) bilabial, (2) labiodental, (3) dental, (4) alveolar, (5) postalveolar, (6) palatal, (7) velar, (8) uvular, (9) pharyngeal, (10) glottal. Most of these terms are simply labels for arbitrarily specified points on the continuum formed by the roof of the mouth and the back wall of the pharynx. As we implied by the empirical observations earlier in this chapter, probably no language requires the specification of more than six of these points at the classificatory level.

Discussion of the feature articulatory place allows us to consider a matter that might have been considered in the discussion of the feature glottal constriction. Both of these features are physiological continua in the sense that they consist of a number of states which can be arranged in a linear order. Thus (7) velar is in some physiological sense between (6) palatal and (8) uvular. In a paper (Ladefoged 1970) which was concerned with the measurement of phonetic similarity for practical purposes such as measuring the mutual intelligibility of different dialects, I suggested that we should distinguish between two kinds of nonbinary features: multivalued scalar features (which would lead to, e.g., e being regarded as between i and a); and multivalued independent features (which would lead to, e.g., p t c k being regarded as being equal phonological distances from each other). It is probably appropriate to consider sounds made at different places of articulation to be equidistant from one another in assessments of mutual intelligibility. But it is by no means clear to me whether in this book, where we are trying to set up phonetic features which will be useful in linguistic descriptions, we should regard the possible places of articulation as a linearly ordered set operating in a scalar feature, or an unordered set within a multivalued independent feature. A good argument in favor of the first alternative has been given by Greenberg (1970), who points out that the statement of the universal constraints on the occurrence of ejectives and implosives in the languages of the world must involve a linear ranking of the possible places of articulation in accordance with their distance from the glottis. He notes that since ejectives are easier to make when there is a comparatively small body of air between the closed glottis and the stop closure, languages tend to have (or tend to develop) alveolar ejectives after velar or uvular ejectives; and bilabial ejectives occur only in languages which already have alveolar and velar or uvular ejectives. Similarly, because implosives are easier to make when there is a larger body of air involved, the reverse order is true for the occurrence of these sounds. In addition, within synchronic descriptions of individual languages, we often need rules that involve adjacent places of articulation; rules in which velars become palatals or labiodentals become bilabials are obvious examples.

There are, however, arguments for the view that places of articulation form an unordered set within a multivalued independent feature. Thus there are many cases in which nonadjacent places of articulation are involved in alternations. The best-known examples are those concerning bilabials and velars. But these are relevant to the point under discussion only if we try to restrict ourselves to accounting for all the alternations which affect place of articulation in terms of a single feature. However some alternations are clearly due to auditory rather than physiological similarities between the sounds in question, and the existence of a linearly ordered set of places of articulation should not prevent us from having crosscutting auditory features in addition.

The acoustic (and hence auditory) similarities between corresponding sounds made in the labial and velar regions is often considerable. The reasons for this acoustic similarity are complex and cannot be given here. It must suffice to say that sounds made with a constriction in either of these areas often have an overtone structure in which most of the acoustic energy is at a lower pitch than in the corresponding sounds made in the alveolar or palatal regions. This effect is greatest for voiceless stops, so that p and k sound more alike than p and t or k and t . But it may also be apparent for voiceless fricatives, where it accounts for the similarity of f and x . This similarity led to the historical change whereby the x which occurred in Old English at the ends of words such as *rough* and *cough* changed to f, in modern English. A lesser but still noticeable similarity of this kind can be observed among voiced stops and fricatives. Following Jakobson (Jakobson, Fant, and Halle 1952; Jakobson 1962) we will refer to this feature as GRAVITY.

It seems probable that we also need another feature, APICALITY, in order to be able to specify the difference between apical and laminal articulations. This feature is irrelevant when neither the tip nor the blade of the tongue is involved. The value 0 may be assigned to sounds made with the absolute tip of the tongue, and the value 1 to articulations involving an arbitrary location considered to be maximally far back on the blade of the tongue. If it is found necessary to specify sounds made with the underpart of the blade (as, for instance, in the phonetic characterization of the extremely retroflex sounds which occur in some Indo-Aryan languages) then negative values could be assigned.

We have already noted that there is little or no evidence for this feature at the classificatory level. Accordingly, it is proper to be hesitant about accepting its necessity at the systematic phonetic level, since it seems that in any one language the use of an apical or a laminal articulation can always be predicted from the values of the other features. If the feature of apicality is required it is not because it is ever used in an unpredictable way to produce contrasts within any one language, but because languages differ from one another in unpredictable ways in their use of this feature. In the first chapter we saw that a phonetic theory must be capable of distinguishing not only all the contrasts that occur within a language, but also all the phonetic events that characterize one language as different from another. Apicality is needed for the latter purpose, since, as table 21 shows, one language (Temne) may use apical dentals and laminal alveolars whereas another (Isoko) is characteristically different in that it uses apical alveolars and laminal dentals.

Finally, as we will see in the chapter on vowels, we also need a feature of tongue shape in order to be able to specify the difference between tense and lax vowels. To make it quite clear that this feature is being defined by reference to the action of the tongue alone, it should be termed tongue tension; but we will follow the usual practice and simply call the feature TENSION. It will be discussed more fully in chapter 8.

Table 25 The oro-nasal process and some articulatory categories

Phonetic term	Brief description	Symbols
Oral	Soft palate raised forming a velic closure; none of the air going out through the nose	ə w b
Nasal	Soft palate lowered so that some or all of the air goes out through the nose	ə̃ w̃ m ŋ͡l
Stop	Complete closure of two articulators	p b m ɕ
Fricative	Narrowing of two articulators so as to produce a turbulent airstream	v s ɬ
Approximant	Approximation of two articulators without producing a turbulent airstream	ə w l ɹ
Trill	One articulator vibrating against another	r ʀ
Tap	One articulator thrown against another	ɾ
Flap	One articulator striking another in passing	ɽ ɭ
Lateral	Articulated so that air passes out at the side	l ɬ ɭ
Central	Articulated so that air passes out in the center	w s ɹ ɫ ɕ

6. Manners Of Articulation

A preliminary list of the manners of articulation is given in table 25. As a matter of convenience in summarizing terms the two possible states of the oro-nasal process are also listed in this table. This list of manners of articulation is clearly insufficient to account for all the linguistic contrasts that occur. But it is useful in that it allows us to begin with a simple model which distinguishes between only three degrees of obstruction to the airstream (complete stoppage, restricted flow, and unimpeded flow; here called stop, fricative, and approximant) and three other gestures (trill, tap, and flap), which occur at a more limited number of places of articulation. For the moment we may consider the approximant category to be simply a convenient general term to include what others have called semivowels, laterals, and frictionless continuants (as well as vowels, which we will consider later).

Within each of the groups of terms in table 25, specification of any one term precludes all the others. If a sound is oral it is not also nasal; if it is a stop, it cannot be simultaneously a fricative, or an approximant, or a trill, or a tap, or a flap; if it is central it cannot be lateral. But between terms in different groups there is a great deal of freedom of combination. All these articulations can be oral or nasal (although, as we have already noted, possibly only stops and approximants contrast in this way at the segmental level); and we shall see that the terms central and lateral can be applied not only to approximants and fricatives, but also to stops and some forms of flaps. Many of these combinations are abbreviated or left not fully specified in traditional phonetic terminology. We have already noted that oral stops and nasal stops are more commonly called simply stops and nasals. Similarly central fricatives and central approximants are usually referred to simply as fricatives and approximants, and lateral approximants are usually called laterals. Generally, combinations are noted only in describing less common phenomena such as lateral fricatives.

Stops and nasals have already been plentifully exemplified, and need not be considered further. But the category fricative requires more discussion for a number of reasons. In the first place it should be noted that the turbulence of the airstream is not necessarily formed at the actual place of articulation — the point at which the two articulators are closest together. The two places coincide in the formation of v ; but in s the principal source of acoustic energy is the turbulence produced when the jet of air, which is formed by the groove between the tongue and the alveolar ridge, strikes the edges of the teeth. Another difference among fricatives is that some are made with the tongue relatively flat in the mouth, whereas others involve the formation of a comparatively narrow groove. Some writers have recognized this by further division of the members of the class which are made with the fore part of the tongue, separating out a class of grooved fricatives (Pike 1943), or rill spirants (Hockett 1955). It is often difficult to decide how to apply this distinction; and it is clearly irrelevant for fricatives made with the lips and the back of the tongue. Nevertheless there are good reasons for thinking that some further division of the fricative category is necessary. A palatographic investigation (Ladefoged 1957) showed that in some people's speech the sounds at the beginnings of the English words *sip* and *ship* were articulated on very similar parts of the alveolar ridge; the consistent difference in these two sounds for all English speakers was not in the place of articulation, but in the face that ʃ was always associated with a wider articulatory channel and more doming (as opposed to hollowing) of the fore part of the tongue. Using only the categories we have established so far, the only way to differentiate between these two sounds, both of which are made with the tip of the tongue in my normal pronunciation, is by calling one apical alveolar and the other apical post-alveolar. But if we do this we cannot differentiate between an apical ʃ and the apical postalveolar which we previously called retroflex. These two sounds may contrast in many Dravidian languages, all of which also have an apical s which is not particularly dental. Kannada and Telugu examples are given in table 26. I have heard a number of Kannada informants who have two sounds almost identical with those in English *sip* and *ship* (except that they do not have the accompanying movements of the lips which normally occur in

Table 26 Contrasts involving apical alveolar, postalveolar, and retroflex fricatives in Kannada and Telugu

	Alveolar	Postalveolar	Retroflex
Kannada	saaku enough	ʃaama black	wiṣa poison
Telugu	maasaw month	aaʃa ambition	kaṣaajaw decoction
	haasjʌ̃w sarcasm	druʃjam scenery	baaṣjʌ̃w commentary

English) as well as a third sound which is a voiceless retroflex fricative with (to me, but not to them) a very similar auditory quality. But the situation is complicated because the difference between the apical ʃ and the apical postalveolar fricative in these Dravidian languages is associated with erudition and a spelling difference. Many people who claim to make the difference do not always do so in their everyday speech.

One way of differentiating between all these fricatives would be to list an additional place of articulation and to regard (apical) postalveolar and (apical) retroflex as distinct categories. But this seems unsatisfactory since this extra place is needed only to account for the fricative sounds which occur, and we have already noted that it is not really the appropriate way of distinguishing among these. Another solution would be to specify the difference between s and ʃ in terms of the secondary articulation of palatalization (to be described later). But this does not account for the differences in the articulatory channel described above. At the moment I am inclined to think that the best solution is to distinguish between grooved and slit fricatives. But perhaps it would be better to admit that we do not have a good way of describing these tongue-tip articulations. This seems even more obvious when we come to examine some of the other problems, such as the difference between ʒ , z , and ɹ , the latter being a voiced apical fricative which is nevertheless not retroflex. These three sounds occur in contrast in some languages (e.g., South African English, where ɹ is the usual form of r). In a previous discussion (Ladefoged 1964a) of Bini, which also has ɹ , I carefully avoided the necessity of specifying this sound in terms of exact categories. We clearly need the results of a good cross-linguistic study of fricatives before we can progress in this area.

A fricative form of trilled r occurs in Czech. This leads us to consider whether the category fricative is really a member of a set of which the other members are stop, approximant (or something equivalent), trill, tap, and flap, or whether it is, like central–lateral, an independent, additive component. What characterizes the Czech variant of the trill manner of articulation is that it is a laminal (and not an apical) trill, and the stricture is held for longer (but probably with a shorter onset and offglide). Accordingly this example does not provide us with good grounds for saying that the category fricative is not a member of the larger set, mutually exclusive with all the other terms. In any case, no language distinguishes between a fricative and a nonfricative trill, and so we have no motivation for introducing this possibility into our scheme of categories. (This does not, of course, dispose of the question whether the category fricative is an independent, additive component or not. We will return to this point later.)

The other manners of articulation are much more restricted in the places of articulation at which they can occur. The majority of trills, taps, and flaps are made with the tip of the tongue. In a trill the tip of the tongue may be loosely held near some part of the roof of the mouth and set in vibration by the action of the airstream in much the same way as the vocal cords are set in motion during the production of voice. In a typical speech sound produced in this way there may be about three vibratory movements; but even in cases where there is only a single contact with the roof of the mouth, the action is physiologically (but perhaps not auditorily) quite distinct from that of a tap. A tap is formed by a single contraction of the muscles such that one articulator is thrown against the other. The distinction between these two gestures is exemplified in table 27 by contrasts in Tamil and Spanish. Educated Tamil also has a voiced postalveolar approximant, so that some speakers have three contrasting sounds similar to the sounds which are all diaphones of r in different forms of English.

Table 27 Contrasts involving alveolar taps and trills in Tamil and Spanish

	Alveolar tap	Alveolar trill	Postalveolar approximant
Tamil	eɾəm	ərəm	aaɻəm
	saw	charity	depth
Spanish	peɾo	pero	
	but	dog	

Apical trills or taps are usually in the dental or alveolar regions. Malayalam is the only language I have investigated which (in some dialects) makes a distinction between two trills in this area, one being more dental and the other more alveolar. A recent palatographic investigation showed that these trills are probably further distinguished by the action of the back of the tongue. These two trills contrast with two laterals and with a retroflex approximant, as shown in table 28.

A flap is an articulation which usually involves the curling of the tip of the tongue up and back and then allowing it to hit the roof of the mouth as it

Table 28 Contrasts involving two different apical trills, a retroflex approximant and an alveolar and a retroflex lateral in Malayalam (suggested by Devidas Narayan)

Advanced alveolar trill	Retracted alveolar trill	Retroflex approximant	Alveolar lateral	Retroflex lateral
ʌ ř ʌ	ʌ ř ʌ	a aɻ ʌ		
half	room	banana tree		
p u ř ʌ	p u ř ʌ	p uɻ ʌ		
roof	outer	river		
k ʌ ř i	k ʌ ř i	k ʌɻ i	k ʌ l i	k ʌ ḷ i
charcoal	curry	skein of yarn	possessed by a spirit	game

returns to a position behind the lower teeth. A flap is therefore distinguished from a tap by having one articulator strike against another in passing while on its way back to its rest position, as opposed to striking immediately after leaving its rest position.

Retroflex flaps are common in Indo-Aryan languages. A distinction between a flap and a tap (which may be allophonically a trill) is made in Hausa. Palatograms and details of the contrast have been published elsewhere (Ladefoged 1964a); examples are given in table 29. Voiceless trills, taps, and flaps are comparatively uncommon; many languages (e.g., Gaelic, Bini) have a voiceless fricative or approximant ɻ̥ , but I have not heard any forms where ɽ̥ or ɾ̥ is the normal variant.

The central–lateral dichotomy may be applied to flaps, but not to taps and trills. There are a number of languages in which sounds having the characteristic gesture involved in making a flap may have in addition a distinctly lateral quality; when the articulation is formed there is contact only

Table 29 Contrast involving a flap and a tap (which may be allophonically a trill) in Hausa

b á ɽ à   servant   b á ɾ à   begging

51

in the center of the mouth, so that momentarily there is a position similar to that of an l . This kind of sound often occurs in languages which do not make a contrast between l and any form of r (e.g., Haya); but it also occurs as a third item contrasting with both l and some form of r in a number of languages. Some Chaga examples are given in table 30.

Table 30 Contrasts involving an alveolar trill, an alveolar lateral flap, and an alveolar lateral approximant in Chaga

r i ha	to mash	ɺi h o	exciting	l i t ʃ a	something good
r i na	a hole	ɺ i ka	hide something		

   The tongue tip is not the only articulator which can be trilled: the uvula can be made to vibrate in a similar way. No language contrasts uvular and lingual trills; nor does any language contrast uvular trills with uvular fricatives and approximants. Different dialectal forms of French use all these possibilities.

   Trills, taps, and flaps may also be made with the lips. Again these three possibilities are not used contrastively. I have heard a voiced bilabial trill or flap in Ngwe, which is in phonemic contrast with m , b , mb (Dunstan 1964), but which occurs only after m . It is therefore a trill generated in a slightly different way from the tongue-tip trill, in that the lips are blown apart by the pressure of the airstream, instead of being held loosely apart and then being sucked together and set into vibratory motion. Other lip actions occur elsewhere. Margi has a kind of labiodental flap, photographs of which have been published elsewhere (Ladefoged 1964a). The articulation is fairly complex and does not fit into any of the categories defined above. The lower lip is first pulled backward against the upper teeth, contact being maintained at the same time with the upper lip. Then there is a downward movement so that the lower lip comes away from the upper lip, slips off the upper teeth, and (because of the backward pull which is being exerted) moves in behind the upper front teeth. As it is brought back from this position to its normal position, it flaps against the upper teeth. A similar sound occurs in Shona; good photographs have been published by Doke (1931). My Shona informants pronounced this sound without the first stage, the tensing of the lower lip against the upper teeth found in Margi; in Shona the lower lip is simply drawn back behind the upper teeth, and then flapped forward with a much looser action. Some words contain two of these flaps in succession. Similar sounds have been reported in other African languages (Westermann and Ward 1933; Tucker 1940). Bilabial trills have also been noted in the Amerindian languages Amuzgo and Isthmus Zapotec (Pike 1963), but in accordance with the general scheme of this book tables 31 and 32 list only Ngwe and Shona examples which I have heard myself. Voiceless varieties of these sounds are reported in Ngwe (Dunstan, personal communication) and some of the non-Bantu languages of North-Eastern Africa (Tucker and Bryan 1966).

Table 31 Contrasts involving a labial trill or flap in Ngwe (suggested by Elizabeth Dunstan Mills). This articulation is here indicated by * .

m*ɤ :   tadpoles   bə̀vɛt   grease
mɑ́fɔ̀ɑ̀   chieftainness   mbɛm   seed

Table 32 Contrasts involving labiodental flaps in Shona (suggested by George Fortune). This articulation is here indicated by * .

ko*ɓ   ideophone indicating blackness
wɓ*o   ideophone indicating movement

The central–lateral opposition is completely independent of the categories specifying manner of articulation. It can be applied to approximants (the ordinary l sound in English is an alveolar lateral approximant; Malayalam retroflex lateral approximants were illustrated in table 28), and to flaps (as in the Chaga examples in table 30) and fricatives (examples of Zulu alveolar lateral fricatives are given in table 33). The contrast between lateral approximants and lateral fricatives occurs only among voiced sounds. I do not know of any language that distinguishes between voiceless lateral fricatives and approximants, although many languages (e.g., Welsh and Burmese; see table 2) have one or the other of these sounds. As is shown in table 33, Zulu has a voiceless alveolar lateral fricative as well as a contrast between a voiced alveolar lateral approximant and fricative. In addition, table 33 includes some items labeled lateral stops. In this label it might appear that the term lateral is being used in an unusual way; but the best way of distinguishing between the sounds at the beginning of the Zulu words for *pound* and *dress up* is by calling one of them an alveolar lateral click and the other an alveolar central click. It is

Table 33 Contrasts involving laterals in Zulu (suggested by L.W. Lanham). All these items are imperative forms of verbs, all with a sequence of low tone followed by high tone.

	Alveolar lateral approximant	Alveolar lateral fricative	Alveolar lateral velaric stop (click)	Palatal lateral glottalic stop (ejective)	Postalveolar central velaric stop (click)
Voiced	l on d a	ɮuɮa	g͡ʒoba		g͡ʟoka
	preserve	roam loose	pound		dress up
Voiceless	ɬoɬa	ʒoʒa	cʌ'ecʌ'a	ʗaʗa
	prod	narrate	tattoo	explain

theoretically possible to regard these items as sequences, but of which segments I am not at all clear. Consequently in practice it seems difficult to avoid applying the terms central and lateral to clicks; and once the practice has been established of regarding certain stop consonants (the clicks) as central or lateral, it seems logical to extend this usage to ejectives (and, in other languages, to implosives and plosives). There is clearly a physiological unity to ejective laterals (such as Zulu cʌ' and the more common t ɭ ' which forms part of the ejective series in many Amerindian languages such as Navaho). It is very difficult to describe these gestures as sequences of two other gestures. So we may regard the central–lateral opposition as an additive component for stops, as well as for fricatives, approximants, and flaps. When used in relation to stops this opposition specifies not just the manner of the sound after the closure, but more especially the place of release of the closure. Although the terms central and lateral were summarized in table 25 along with other terms such as stop, trill, and fricative, we must remember that central and lateral really form an independent set, just as much related to the terms specifying the place of articulation as to those specifying the manner.

Lateral articulations probably occur only with the dental, alveolar, retroflex, and palatal categories of articulation. Velar laterals are reported in some Malayo-Polynesian languages, but I have heard only voiced velar fricatives or approximants in the languages of this group which might have this sound (e.g., Aklanon). Investigators may be tempted to imagine that this sound is a lateral simply because in neighboring languages there is an l in cognate words. Similarly many dialects of English have a sound which occurs where other dialects have a postvocalic l , but which in these dialects involves no central contact between the tongue and the roof of the mouth. This sound will be discussed in the next section, when the secondary articulation of velarization is considered.

It would be difficult to find a single feature underlying all the manners of articulation we discussed earlier. But it is equally obvious that these are not all separate, unrelated phenomena, which have to be described by a set of binary features, each indicating virtually only presence or absence of an event. We must account for the fact that, for example, fricatives are more related to stops than stops are to vowels. It might seem as if the most appropriate way of handling this relationship would be to set up a feature which could be called articulatory stricture. This feature would have three principal values, corresponding to the degrees of articulatory stricture in stops, fricatives, and approximants. These values would form a linearly ordered set, by means of which we could give an explanatory account of lenition phenomena, in which stops weaken to fricatives, and a further weakening gives rise to approximants.

The difficulty with this solution is that it does not permit the category fricative to co-occur with the category stop; and unless we do this we have no way of showing that affricates are related to both fricatives and stops. Alternations involving stops becoming affricates, and these affricates becoming fricatives seem just as natural as the lenition phenomena cited above. If we regard affrication as a separate feature which may or may not occur with stops, then we cannot (without extra rules) show that affricates are simply related to fricatives.

On the whole, therefore, it seems best to regard the two processes of lenition, one in going from stop to fricative and the other in going from fricative to approximant, as different from each other. Instead we will set up two independent features STOP and FRICATIVE. Affricates will be considered to have positive values for both features, and approximants to have zero values for both features. This solution is unsatisfactory in that it makes stops and fricatives both equally different from approximants (they both differ by only one term); but it is the best that can be done unless we add a feature which we might call strength (cf. Foley 1970a, 1970b), which would have values similar to those proposed for articulatory stricture above. There is evidence (George Papçun, personal communication) that such a feature might have some experimental validity. But for the moment we will leave this as an open question.

This leaves us with trills, taps, and flaps to consider. Clearly, these sounds must be distinguished both from stops, fricatives, and approximants and from each other. As a first step in doing this it is appropriate to set up an additional feature, which we will call VIBRATION, and to classify trills and taps as having a positive value of this feature.

The distinction between trills and taps is the same as that between stops and flaps, and requires an additional feature which we may call RATE. Most sounds can be said to have a normal (or 0) value on this scale. But when an articulation such as a stop occurs more rapidly, it may be specified by a higher value. The flapped sounds which occur in Hausa and in some Indian languages might be assigned a value of more than 0, say +1, on this arbitrary scale. Similarly the short movement which occurs in a tap as in Spanish *pero* may be considered to be a more rapid version of the Spanish trill in *perro*, and may be assigned a value of +1. A feature of this kind seems to capture the correct relationship between stops and flaps in that it allows us to state that a stop (as in American English *rat*) may become a flap (as in *ratty*) by a simple increase in the rate feature which occurs in a given environment. In addition it shows the similarity between taps and trills. These sounds sometimes contrast (as in Spanish), but they more often alternate or are in free variation (as, for example, in Hausa and some forms of Scottish English). Furthermore, it may be possible to use this feature to describe other contrasts between sounds which are due to differences in articulatory rate. Thus the difference between vowels and semivowels can be described in this way, semivowels being given a positive value as for a flap or a tap. But what is far more important is that all contrasts in length can be described in terms of this feature. Sounds which are some arbitrary percentage longer than normal may be assigned a value of - 1; and lower values may be assigned to sounds which are even longer, as will be described in a later chapter. This is a useful generalization of a feature, and it is insightful in that it shows that semivowels, taps, and flaps cannot be long, but stops, fricatives, and trills can be involved in contrasts of length.

The four features − stop, fricative, vibration, and rate − will account for most manners of articulation. But in addition we need to distinguish between central and lateral articulations, which we may do by a feature of LATERALITY. It is difficult to conceive what might be meant by in-between values for this feature. At the systematic phonemic level sounds either are lateral or they are not (in which case they are central); and the same seems to be true at the phonetic level.

Finally, as for places of articulation, we must consider whether there are any manners of articulation which we wish to group together because of their auditory similarity. Such groupings would be completely independent of those established in terms of physiological criteria. They might be used to produce further subdivisions of the present physiological classes, or they could result in a separate, crosscutting classification. It should be emphasized yet again that languages work in terms of both the physiological and the acoustic properties of sounds, and one does not want a monosystemic approach to the task of constructing phonological classifications.

The most important example of the useful division of a physiological category in terms of auditory criteria is the division of fricatives into sibilants and nonsibilants. (We may note that the feature fricative is itself dependent on acoustic criteria in its definition, the definitional property turbulence being an acoustic characteristic.) We have already seen that it is difficult to give good physiological descriptions of the differences between members of the category fricative. But it seems quite clear that languages often contain rules which require the distinction between two kinds of fricatives. Thus in English the plural suffix is ɪ z (or something similar, depending on the dialect) after s , z , ʃ , ʒ (and the corresponding affricates) but s or z after other sounds. We could try to define the common factor underlying these sounds in terms of a physiological feature. But this would be not only difficult, but also inappropriate, as it would lead us to overlook the real explanation of why these sounds act together as a class, which is that they have a great deal of auditory similarity. Fricatives such as s and ʃ are distinguished from others by having a comparatively large amount of acoustic energy at high frequencies. Sounds with an acoustic structure of this kind may be said to have the auditory feature SIBILANCE.

At the systematic phonemic level sounds are either sibilant or not; but at the phonetic level they may vary in their degree of sibilance. If we are thinking simply in terms of phonetic symbols, it is impossible to be precise over which represents a sibilant and which does not. Languages differ so that a given sound may have to be classed among the sibilants in one language, whereas in another language its sibilance may be ignored in comparison with that of some other more strikingly sibilant sound. The relative nature of these auditory contrasts should not be in any way surprising. We have already discussed a very similar situation for the physiologically defined feature voice onset, where we saw that a sound that in one language might be regarded as a voiceless (unaspirated) stop might in another language be considered the voiced counterpart of an aspirated stop. In the case of the auditory feature sibilance we are handicapped because we do not know how to make acoustic measurements that can be correlated with the perceptual characteristics of this feature. The correct weight which should be given to variations in overall acoustic intensity in comparison with the intensity in a particular high frequency region is as yet undetermined; but there is no doubt that there is a perceptual scale such that sounds can vary in their degree of sibilance.

The other auditory features which may be needed in phonological classifications do not have the effect of subdividing groups of sounds which have been established in terms of physiological criteria. Instead they permit us to combine sounds which have little in common from a physiological point of view. As more and more becomes known about the classes of sounds required in the rules of a wide variety of languages, linguists will almost certainly find that they have to posit several additional features of this kind; but in this preliminary survey we will illustrate only one.

In many languages sounds such as those at the ends of the words *table, sudden, prism,* and *hinder* act together as a class. Thus in English these sounds are syllabic after a stop or a fricative, as in the words cited above, but not (for most of us) in a word such as *film.* The sounds which behave in this way are called sonorants, as opposed to stops and fricatives which are nonsonorants or obstruents. We will use the term SONORANT for a particular group of sounds, which we will define as those sounds with an auditory property which arises from their having a comparatively large amount of acoustic energy within a clearly defined formant structure (a term which will be discussed in more detail in chapter 8, when we consider vowels).

7. Secondary Articulation

Sounds can also be modified by secondary articulations which occur at the same time as the primary articulations. Following Pike (1943) we will consider a secondary articulation to have a lesser degree of stricture than the primary articulation, and to be made with articulators left free by the primary articulation. But, unlike Pike, we will also consider sounds which have two equal articulatory strictures at different places of articulation to consist of a primary articulation which is closer to the glottis and a secondary articulation which is further away from it. By the end of this chapter we will have reverted to an analysis which is fairly similar to Pike's; but for purposes of exposition it is convenient to modify his definition so that it includes double articulations.

We will consider the double articulations (two equal degrees of stricture) first. All of them involve the action of the lips, which (since they must be farther from the glottis than the other stricture) will be regarded as the secondary articulators. We shall use the terms labial-velar, labial-palatal, and labial-alveolar when describing these sounds, restricting the form labio- to the term labiodental, which specifies an articulation involving only one lip.

Labial-velars can involve simultaneous stop, fricative, nasal, or approximant articulations. The approximant (semivowel) w in English and many other languages is the most familiar labial-velar sound. Labial-velar stops, nasals, and fricatives occur in West African languages, as I have described in detail elsewhere (Ladefoged 1964a). The stops and nasals are usually symbolized by the bilabial and velar symbols joined together by a tie bar, to indicate that the articulations are simultaneous and not sequential. Examples of contrasts in Idoma are given in table 34. When there is a contrast between a labial-velar approximant and a labial-velar fricative it may be symbolized by adding the diacritic which indicates a closer articulation to the symbol for the approximant. Margi examples of this kind (and of the contrast between a palatal approximant and a palatal fricative) are given in table 35.

Table 34 Contrasts involving labial-velar, labial, and velar stops and nasals in Idoma (suggested by Robert Armstrong; cf. Ladefoged 1964a). The tie mark over two symbols indicated a simultaneous articulation.

àk͡pá	bridge	àpá	lizard	àka	wheel
àg͡bá	jaw	àbá	palm nut	àga	ax
aŋ͡màa	painted body marks	áma	bell	ɔŋáɟi	Western rainbow

59

Table 35 Contrasts involving palatal approximants and fricatives, and labial-velar approximants and fricatives in Margi (from Ladefoged 1964*a*, suggested by Hoffman 1963). The diacritic ^ indicates a closer (and hence fricative) version of the preceding sound.

jà give birth   j^àj^àdò picked up   káwà sorry   w^á reach inside

The contrast between a labial-palatal and a labial-velar approximant occurs in French (examples in table 36). Labial-palatal approximants occur in a number of other languages (e.g., Idoma and Kamba). But I do not know of any examples of labial-palatal stops or nasals. The Shona "whistling fricatives" illustrated in table 37 may exemplify another manner of sound made with this secondary articulation; these sounds may, however, be more properly called labial-alveolars.

Table 36 Contrasts involving palatal, labial-palatal, and labial-velar approximants in French.

Palatal		**Labial-palatal**		**Labial-velar**	
mjɛt	crumb	mɥɛt	mute	mwɛt	sea gull
lje	tied	lɥi	him	lwi	Louis
		ɥit	eight	wi	yes

Table 37 Contrasts involving the "whistling fricatives" (here symbolized ɕ͡w ʑ͡w in Shona. In going from s to ɕ͡w to ɕ there is increasing retardation and flattening of the tongue (examples suggested by George Fortune).

(Apical) alveolar		**Labial-(laminal) alveolar**		**(Laminal) prepalatal**	
màsóró	big heads	ɕ͡wòɕ͡wé	sugar ant	mùɕòmà	be hoarse
màzòrò	turns	ʑ͡wósé	all	ʑòʑómá	tuft of hair
tsámà	handful	ɾt͡ɕ͡wá	new thing	t̪ɕáná	fat child
dzámá	disappear	ɾd͡ʑ͡wá	new thing	d̪ʑànà	turn

The only other labial-alveolars I have heard are stops or nasals. They occur in West African languages, often (as in Dagbani) as allophonically predictable variants of the more common labial-velars, but in some languages (such as Bura, illustrated in table 38) as the only series of double articulations. I have not heard any contrasts between labial-alveolars and labial-velars, but they are reported by Chinebuah (1962) in Nzima.

Table 38 Contrasts involving labials and labial-alveolars in Bura (suggested by Carl Hoffmann; cf. Ladefoged 1964a).

p à k à	search	p̂ t á	hare
p s á	lay eggs	p̂ t s à	roast
p ʃ à r ì	spread a net	p̂ t ʃ i	sun
b a ɬ a	dance	b̂ d à	chew

Many other secondary articulations with two equal degrees of stricture are possible. An alveolar-velar fricative has been reported in some dialects of Swedish (Abercrombie 1967), and I have heard what might be labiodental-postalveolar fricatives in Kutep (illustrated by X-ray data in Ladefoged 1964a). But I am not sure if these sounds really have two equal articulations, each producing a turbulent airstream. There are more obviously two articulations in the Shona nasals written *ny*. Both my own palatograms and those of Doke (1931) show that there are two contacts – a tongue tip (or blade) and alveolar ridge contact, and probably simultaneously, a tongue front and hard palate contact. But these contacts are probably best considered to be due to accidents of the shapes involved; in trying to make palatal nasals speakers fail to get the front of the tongue to make contact in the midpalatal area of the hard palate, and settle for alveolar and postpalatal contact instead.

The most important secondary articulations in which one articulatory stricture is less than the other are movements toward and away from an approximant position occurring simultaneously with the formation and release of another articulation. Some secondary articulations of this kind which may be needed to account for linguistic contrasts are listed in table 39. (It should be remembered that nasalization and phonation types such as laryngealization are not articulations, and therefore are not considered here.)

Labialization, an approximation or rounding of the lips, may be exemplified as the main distinguishing feature in several pairs of sounds in

Table 39 Some secondary articulations

Phonetic term	Brief description	Symbols
Labialization	Added lip-rounding or protrusion	sᵂ , bᵂ , tᵂ
Palatalization	Raising of the front of the tongue	sʲ , bʲ , tʲ
Velarization	Raising of the back of the tongue	sˠ , bˠ , tˠ
Pharyngealization	Retracting of the root of the tongue	sˤ , bˤ , tˤ

Akan languages, as in the Twi examples shown in table 40. It is also a component of the pronunciation of r , ʃ , and other consonants in many forms of English. For typographic reasons labialized sounds are here specified by a small ᵂ ; it is difficult to put a diacritic under or over a symbol such as ʃ . But it should be noted that not only is there no intention of indicating a sequence, but also the symbol ᵂ indicates simply a labial articulation, not a labial-velar articulation.

Table 40 Contrasts involving labialization in Asante Twi (suggested in part by Paul Schachter; see also Ladefoged 1964a).

càcà	straw mattress	òcᵂá?	he cuts
òɟá	he leads	òɟᵂá	he carves
òɲá	he finds	ɲᵂá	snail
ɔʃɛ	he puts on	ɔʃᵂɛ	he looks at

We may note here that it may be necessary to consider two different kinds of lip rounding. It is possible to form a small lip aperture by bringing the corners of the mouth forward and protruding the lips; or it can be done by closing the jaw and bringing the lips together vertically, so that the side portions are in contact, but there is a gap in the center. Sweet (1890) called these two possibilities inner rounding and outer rounding; Heffner (1950) uses the terms horizontal lip rounding and vertical lip rounding; perhaps a better pair of terms might be lip rounding (which would include protrusion) as opposed to lip compression. Kelly (1966) has shown that the distinction occurs in Urhobo, which has (in addition to labiodental and labial-velar fricatives ʋ and wˆ) both labial-velar and labial approximants. Kelly points out that this latter sound, which was symbolized ʋ in the Urhobo examples in Ladefoged

(1964a), is accompanied by the tongue position of the adjacent vowels; so when it occurs with high back vowels, it is distinguishable from the labial-velar approximant w only because the lip gesture involves (vertical) compression as opposed to (horizontal) rounding and protrusion.

Several sounds which are often said to be labialized are sequences of partially overlapping articulations. Thus the beginning of the word *quick* clearly involves a sequence in that the lip rounding in a phrase such as *pretty quick* is not coterminous with the formation and release of the closure; and although both the formation and release of the stop consonant in *see two* may be accompanied by lip rounding, the peak in the labial activity is always much nearer the latter. Both the stop in *quick* and that in *two* can be described in terms of a sequence of items. At the phonetic level they do not involve simultaneous secondary articulations of the kind that occurs in the initial constants in *rick* and *ship*. But of course from a phonological point of view it may be advisable to consider some stops of this kind as being units involving a secondary articulation.

Palatalization is another well-known secondary articulation. It consists of a high front vowellike articulation which usually occurs very slightly after the consonant, and which has much shorter durational characteristics than those associated with a normal vowel. Palatalization is a well-known feature of Russian and other Slavic languages; examples are given in table 41.

Table 41 Contrasts involving palatalization in Russian

brat	brother	brat^j	to take
krɔf	roof	krɔf^j	blood
stal	he has become	stal^j	steel
ʒar	beat	ʒar^j	cook

Velarization and pharyngealization are also vowellike gestures of part of the tongue, the former being associated with the raising of the back of the tongue, and the latter with its retraction. No language uses a contrast between these two possibilities: but contrasts between one or the other of them and palatalized sounds do occur. Thus it is said that some older speakers of Polish make a contrast between a velarized and a palatalized lateral. The younger Polish speakers I have heard do not have this contrast.

In Berber languages the distinction between emphatic and nonemphatic consonants is largely that the former are velarized or pharyngealized, whereas the latter are not; Tamazight examples are given in table 42. In these languages (and in Arabic) the effect is certainly as noticeable on the subsequent vowel as on the consonant itself, and the secondary articulation cannot be said to be coterminous with the consonant, or with any other segment.

A well-known example of velarization occurs in many forms of British English where the ł phoneme has two extrinsic allophones. For syllable initial l the tip of the tongue touches the alveolar ridge and the rest of the tongue assumes the position required for the following vowel, except that there is a

Table 42 Contrasts involving velarization or pharyngealization or both in Tamazight (suggested by Jeanette Johnson Harries; cf. Johnson 1966)

i b ð̆a t	he began it	i b ð̆$^\text{ʢ}$a t	he divided it
t a ʒ r	rich man	t$^\text{ʢ}$a ʒ i n	stew
z u r n	they are fat	z$^\text{ʢ}$u r n	they made a pilgrimage
i r s a	he dismounted	i r s$^\text{ʢ}$a	he quieted down

narrowing of the tongue so that there is no contact at one or both sides; but in syllable final ł or syllabic ļ the back of the tongue is raised so that there is strong velarization. In some forms of British English (such as London English or my own debased RP), there is no alveolar contact and the tip of the tongue is behind the lower front teeth for the syllable final ł and syllabic ļ ; but the back of the tongue is still raised, and there is still a narrowing of the tongue such that, if there were central alveolar contact, the sound would be a lateral. The problem is how to classify this articulation. The raising of the back of the tongue cannot be called a secondary articulation when there is no other stricture; and although the narrowing of the tongue is still present, the sound is not a lateral. For the moment we must leave this phonetic problem unresolved.

There are several possible ways in which the secondary articulations we have been discussing could be incorporated into a feature system. In the first place we could add two features, the manner of secondary articulation and the place of secondary articulation. Thus when describing each sound we could say what kind of secondary articulation was involved, presumably using a feature with three possible values – none, approximant, and stop – and another specifying the place in terms of the five possibilities – nowhere, bilabial, palatal, velar, and pharyngeal. This does not seem entirely appropriate, since the bilabial secondary articulation is the only one which is a truly independent additive component in the sense that its manner of articulation can vary. In addition we must allow for the possibility of sounds being both labialized and palatalized, as occurs in Twi.

Before we go any further in our consideration of secondary articulations it is useful to summarize all the actions of the lips that we have to take into account within a feature system. There seems to be the following set of facts. (1) We need the term labial as a member of the set of possible places of articulation, along with alveolar, velar, and so on. (2) As we saw in chapter 5, we need the feature gravity to show that some labial sounds are more related to the corresponding velar sounds than to those made at other places of articulation. (3) In many languages there are rules that show that labial consonants are more related to rounded than to unrounded vowels. Thus in Turkish (Lees 1961) labial consonants give rise to rounded vowels in circumstances where unrounded vowels would have been predicted by other rules. (4) Labial consonants, just like other consonants, can have added lip-rounding which may be contrastive. Thus in Luganda there are contrasts such as ˈmbʷa̋ 'dog' and ˈmba̋a̋la 'termite' in which the labialized bilabials are subject to the same rules concerning vowel length and tone as other labialized stop consonants. (5) Labialization (rounding) must be distinguished from labial compression, both of which occur in Urhobo (Kelly 1966) and Isoko (Ladefoged 1964*a*). (6) Labial-velars must be more related to both labials and velars than to, say, alveolars. As we shall show directly, the best way of doing this is by making labial-velar an additional term in the set of places of articulation and relating labial-velars to labials and velars by means of the feature gravity. (7) At least on the phonetic level, labial-velars can be labialized. In Nupe, which is a member of the only group of languages in which there are systematic phonetic contrasts between labialized and nonlabialized labial-velars, these contrasts have been shown (Hyman 1970) to be due to an elided vowel in the underlying forms. But this is irrelevant to the fact that at the phonetic level there must be some mechanism for showing the possibility.

These points can be handled only by having two additional places of articulation and another feature. We shall therefore add to the ten terms given on page   for the feature articulatory place the two further terms (11) labial-velar and (12) labial-alveolar. We will also define a feature ROUNDING as the extent to which the corners of the lips are pulled forward and together. At the systematic phonemic level this seems to be a binary contrast; but at the systematic phonetic level sounds obviously differ in degree of rounding. Examples of the classification of a number of the sounds we have been discussing are given in table 43.

Table 43 Examples of the classification of sounds in terms of some of the features discussed so far

	b	d	g	u	i	bʷ	g͡b	β	v	wˆ	g͡bʷ	d͡b	w	y
Place	1	4	7	7	6	1	11	1	2	11	11	12	11	6
Grave	+	−	+	+	−	+	+	+	+	+	+	+	+	−
Round	−	−	−	+	−	+	−	−	−	+	+	−	+	+

We will postpone discussion of the features we need to account for the other secondary articulations, palatalization, velarization, and pharyngealization, since they all require specifications similar to those which will be needed for vowel sounds.

8.   Vowels

The description of vowels in terms of a limited number of categories raises a number of problems, some of which I have discussed at length elsewhere (Ladefoged 1964b, 1967). In general we can say that vowels can be described as points on a continuum in a way that is not true for consonants (with the possible exception of the categories for place of articulation). Our first task is to attempt to define the parameters which specify the vowel continuum. For the past hundred years the traditional way of doing this has nominally been in terms of the position of the highest point of the tongue and the position of the lips. The disadvantage of this system is that the terms are often not in accord with the physiological facts.

We may begin discussing possible articulatory descriptions of vowels by reference to some of the vowels of Ngwe (Dunstan 1964, 1967), examples of which are given in table 44. This is convenient partly because these vowels represent a wide range of phonetic qualities, eight of which are fairly similar to the well-known cardinal vowels (Jones 1956), and partly because we have good data available (Ladefoged 1964a) which enables us to draw accurate diagrams of the articulatory positions as shown in figure 8. Phoneticians have not stated how they would locate the highest point of the tongue; the most suitable way seems to be by presuming that the lower surfaces of the upper teeth form a horizontal plane. (Approximations usually have to be made because the teeth are seldom on a single plane; but this method works better than using the most nearly flat part of the palate as a reference line, since the majority of subjects have a more curved palate than this particular subject.) The upper part of figure 8 shows the relation between the highest points of the tongue determined in this way. It is apparent that the four front vowels lie on a straight line and may be appropriately specified by the traditional labels. But

Table 44   Some of the vowel contrasts in Ngwe (suggested by Elizabeth Dunstan Mills; cf. Dunstan 1964, 1967, where it is shown that æ is an allophone of ɛ)

1.	mb i	cowries	5.	mb ɑ	person
2.	mb e	knife	6.	mb ɔ	god
3.	mb ɛ	sheath	7.	mb o	hands
4.	mb æ h	pepper	8.	mb u	corners

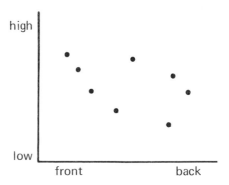

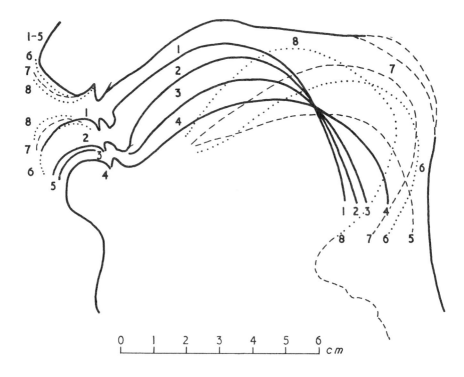

Fig. 8. The articulation involved in the eight Ngwe vowels in table 44. The lower diagram (from Ladefoged 1964a) is based on tracings from single frames of a cineradiology film. The upper diagram shows the relations between the "highest points of the tongue" in these articulations.

the four back vowels have very different tongue shapes from the front vowels, and these tongue shapes can be considered as differing simply in terms of the single parameter called tongue height only be neglecting large and varied differences in the front-back dimension. Moreover, although these four back vowels may not be absolutely identical with the cardinal vowels ɑ ɔ o u , they are certainly fairly similar and form a series of approximately equal auditory steps; but the highest points of the tongue are far from equidistant.

The only way of regarding the articulatory positions of the back vowel as being approximately equidistant is by reference to the position of the point of maximum constriction of the vocal tract. This point, which was suggested as a reference point by Stevens and House (1955), gets progressively farther away from the glottis by roughly equal steps on a logarithmic scale as one goes from ɑ to u . It is thus an appropriate way of specifying back vowels, just as tongue height provides a useful description of front vowels. But specification of tongue shape in terms of the position of the point of maximum constriction is very misleading when applied to front vowels. There is, for instance, no articulatory or acoustic discontinuity corresponding to the discontinuity in this form of specification which occurs when one goes from ɛ (in which the maximum constriction is near the hard palate) to æ (in which it is nearer the pharynx; see fig. 8). There seems to be no single simple set of parameters which is equally appropriate for specifying the tongue shapes of all these vowels.

The vowels shown in figure 8 are in no way exceptional. There are similar difficulties in specifying the position of the highest point of the tongue in the only published X-ray data on a complete set of cardinal vowels (Jones 1929). In these vowels, as in the Ngwe examples, there are great differences in the general shape of the tongue in the set of front vowels and in the set of back vowels, as well as anomalous positions of the highest point of the tongue in back vowels. Similar remarks apply to all the other sets of X-ray data that I have seen. Considering all these difficulties, it is difficult to understand how phoneticians could persist in considering that the traditional articulatory categories provide an adequate specification of vowels.

Some phoneticians have suggested additional articulatory features for specifying the shape of the tongue, such as narrow and wide (Sweet 1890) and tense and lax (Jakobson and Halle 1964). There are certainly grounds for believing that the highest point of the tongue or the point of maximum constriction of the vocal tract (in makes no difference which we consider in this discussion) can be in a given place, but the tongue can be more or less bunched up lengthways (in the anterior posterior dimension). In general, as Lindblom and Sundberg (1969) have shown, the height of the tongue is largely dependent on the position of the jaw. In English and Swedish, and in the Ngwe vowels shown in figure 8, when we take into account the way the jaw is hinged, we can see that the shape of the tongue is much the same in each of the front vowels. But as Sweet pointed out very clearly, it is possible to produce a particular height of the tongue with either a certain jaw position and a relatively flattened tongue, or a lower jaw position and a bunched up tongue; bunching the tongue by pulling the root of it forward toward the mandible results in the main mass of the body of the tongue being displaced upward. Figure 9 (adapted from Ladefoged 1964a) shows the tongue positions in two pairs of Igbo vowels which have similar tongue heights, but which are distinguished by the extent to which the root of the tongue is pulled forward.

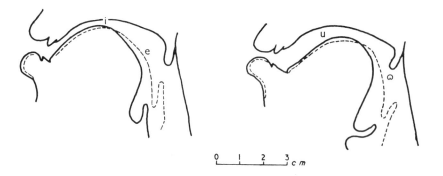

Fig. 9. Tracings from single frames in a cineradiology film showing the articulations involved in the last vowel in each of the Igbo words: óbi , ồbé , íbu , ɔbồ , *heart, poverty, effort, boast.* (From Ladefoged 1964a)

Finally, in considering the articulatory characteristics of vowels we must note that the degree of lip rounding is an independent variable. There is a tendency in the languages of the world for front vowels to be unrounded and back vowels to have lip rounding increasing with tongue height, as in the primary cardinal vowels. But a great many languages have front rounded vowels (usually with greater lip rounding for higher vowels); and several have back unrounded vowels (usually with greater lip spreading for the higher vowels). Examples of front rounded vowels in French are given in table 45; and back unrounded vowels in Mandarin Chinese are exemplified in table 46. Malmberg (1956) has suggested that the difference between what we have called (horizontal) lip rounding with protrusion and (vertical) lip compression may be contrastive in Swedish.

Table 45 Contrasts involving front rounded vowels in French

v i	life	v y	seen	v u	you
d e	thimble	d ø	two	d o	back

Table 46 Contrasts involving back rounded and unrounded vowels in Mandarin Chinese

t s ʰ ɯ	times	s ɯ	four
t s ʰ ù	vinegar	s ù	speed

A convenient way of diagramming the vowel continuum is shown in figure 10. It may be seen that the cardinal vowels do not lie on a single surface of this space; and we must also remember that the terms for the tongue positions are simply traditional labels, which are not easily correlated with the articulatory facts. The three-dimensional continuum has been drawn as if viewed from this particular angle because the individual vowels may then be more easily correlated with the acoustic parameters. So far in this survey of sound types we have not had to consider their acoustic structure in detail. In descriptions of vowels, although a pseudoarticulatory terminology may provide an adequate set of labels for auditory descriptions, we have seen that we do not have, as yet, a set of articulatory parameters which will specify vowel quality. Accordingly, we must consider whether the vowel continuum can be better described in terms of acoustic parameters.

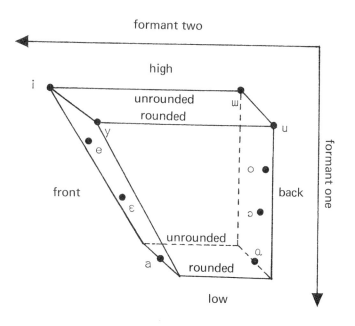

Fig. 10. The (pseudo) articulatory vowel continuum and its relation to formant frequencies.

The basic acoustic data are the frequencies of the formants which characterize each vowel. Roughly speaking, we can say that the sound of a vowel consists of the pitch on which it is said (which is due to the rate of vibration of the vocal cords) and the pitches of the two or three principal groups of overtones (which can be associated with the resonant frequencies of the vocal tract). These groups of overtones are called formants; they are the principal determiners of vowel quality. (See Ladefoged 1962 for an elementary account of formants and acoustic phonetics.) The frequencies (roughly, pitches) of the formants of the vowels in some English (RP) words are shown schematically in the lower part of figure 11. If these vowels are whispered (so that there is no pitch which can be associated with the action of the vocal cords), the falling pitch of formant two can be heard quite easily. If they are said with a creaky voice quality (laryngealized phonation) the rising, then falling pitch of formant one is often apparent. The variations in formant three cannot be demonstrated in any simple way.

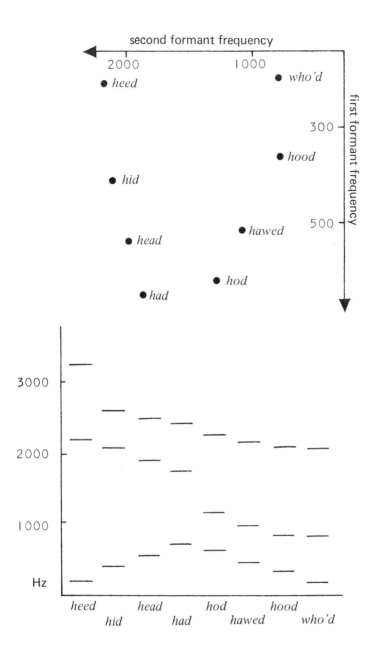

Fig. 11. A formant chart showing the relation between some English (RP) words; and a schematic spectrogram showing the first three formants of the vowels in these words.

A common method of plotting formant frequencies is shown in the upper part of figure 11. Sometimes only the first two formants (F1 and F2) are represented, as here, and sometimes more elaborate combinations involving the third formant (F3) are plotted, such as (F1 + F3) against (F3 − F2). But apart from the work of Jakobson, Fant, and Halle (1952), which will be discussed shortly, there has been very little attempt to locate three or more independently varying acoustic qualities of vowels; and all the two-dimensional plots lead to difficulties. There is no way of giving a two-dimensional specification of front rounded and back unrounded vowels which does not involve some confusion with centralized vowels with other lip positions. If the first formant is plotted against the second, the point for the secondary cardinal vowel y will be very close to that for the vowel in the English word *hid*, as might be inferred from the view of the vowel continuum shown in figure 10.

On the whole, the traditional phonetic descriptions of vowels cannot be more simply interpreted in acoustic terms than in articulatory terms. It is true that the label "vowel height" correlates very nicely with the frequency of the first formant (low vowels having a high first formant, and vice versa). For both front and back vowels a measurement of the first formant frequency will enable one to predict the way a linguist would specify the vowel height, whereas, as we have seen, there is no single articulatory measurement which can be used in a similar way for both these groups of vowels. But measurements of formant frequencies are not so simply related to the other traditional labels, front−back, and spread−round (neglecting, for the moment, tense−lax). The best approximation is that suggested by Fant (personal communication) and reproduced here as figure 12. It may be seen that both front−back and spread−round involve changes in both the first formant and the second and third formants (which are represented together as F2′ in the figure). Consequently even this figure does not really explain what a linguist is doing when he assigns a unique specification to a vowel in terms of the three dimensions high−low, front−back, and spread−round. It is possible that if the acoustic specifications included the formant amplitudes as well as their frequencies we might be able to correlate them more simply with the traditional (auditory) terms. But more research is needed to decide this issue.

In view of the complicated relationships between the traditional terms and any of the possible sets of measurements, we might well wonder whether these terms provide the most appropriate basis for phonological features. But there seems to be no doubt not only that linguists do manage to use these labels in a reliable way, but also that languages work in terms of them. For the moment,

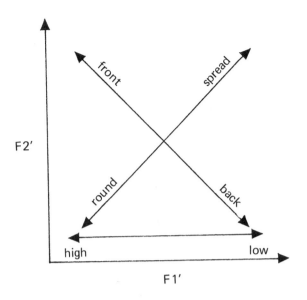

Fig. 12. The relation between the traditional terms for describing vowels and some acoustic parameters (suggested by Fant). F1 is the frequency of the first formant and F2 is a weighted average of the frequencies of the second and third formants.

therefore, we will say that vowels should be described in terms of four features: HEIGHT (the inverse of the frequency of the first formant); BACKNESS (the degree to which the tongue approaches the soft palate or the back wall of the pharynx); ROUNDING (the position of the lips); and TENSION (the degree to which the root of the tongue is pulled forward so that the tongue is bunched up lengthways).

It should be noted that tension is not a completely independent feature. A low back vowel (a vowel with a high first formant, and with the tongue approaching the back wall of the pharynx) can be produced only by contracting the muscles which oppose those that pull the root of the tongue forward; consequently such a vowel cannot be tense in the technical sense defined here. Similarly, although an extreme high front vowel can be produced

75

without pulling the root of the tongue forward, it is certainly much easier to make such a vowel with a tense tongue position that with a lax one.

As we have noted, there are also very frequent correlations between the features of rounding and height, such that high vowels tend to have more extremes of rounding or lip spreading; and there is also a strong tendency for back vowels to be rounded. Neither of these facts is really explained by the vowel features as we have defined them. Both are probably due to some kind of principle of maximal distinctiveness whereby the auditory differences between the vowels in a language tend to be kept at a maximum. We will probably be able to express this principle elegantly only when we can make entirely acoustic descriptions of vowels which will allow us to categorize each different vowel uniquely in terms of a multidimensional auditory space. Meanwhile we must continue with this mixed system involving both auditory and physio-logical specifications.

It is difficult to say how many possible contrasts there are within each of these features, because the vowels of a language usually differ in more than one feature. But we appear to need four degrees of vowel height to account for the Danish and English vowels shown in table 47. For the English vowels it is arguable that the difference between the vowels in the last two words is one of lip rounding rather than height. But at least in my own speech, although there undoubtedly is a difference in rounding, there is also a clear difference in height; and it is phonologically preferable to regard the rounding as determined by the height rather than vice versa, so that one can say that the relationship between ɑ and ɔ is the same as that between ɔ and o and that between o and u .

I cannot find any clear-cut cases of three vowels within a language which contrast just by being front, central, and back, with all other features remaining

Table 47 Contrasts illustrating four degrees of vowel height in Danish and English (RP)

Danish		English	
vi:ðə	know	huʷtə	hooter
ve:ðə	wheat	moʷtə	motor
vɛ:ða	wet (vb)	dɔtə	daughter
væ:ðə	wade	fɑðə	father

the same. But there are a number of cases such as that in Ngwe, illustrated in table 48, where it is certainly convenient to postulate the existence of a category central, which is neither front nor back. There are also often phonological reasons for saying that in languages which have a five-vowel system, and in many of those with a seven-vowel system, the lowest vowel is neither front nor back, and is therefore presumably central. It is arguable that a similar situation obtains in English with respect to the starting points of the diphthongs in *high* and *how*. Despite the rules in Chomsky and Halle (1968), for most people these diphthongs have the same or very similar starting points, and a generalization is lost if one is not able to express this because of inadequacies of the feature system.

Table 48 Examples of contrasts involving central vowels in Ngwe (suggested by Elizabeth Dunstan Mills; cf. Dunstan 1966, 1967, where it is shown that y and ə are allophones of i and ɤ respectively)

	Front	Central	Back	
Rounded	n t y advise		m b u corners	High
Unrounded	mb i cowries	mb ɨ dog		
		n t s ə water	m b ɤ ivory	Mid

There are also no clear-cut cases of three degrees of rounding, although, as we have noted, Malmberg (1956) has suggested that there may be two different kinds of rounding in Swedish (exemplified in table 49). The discussion in the previous chapter showed how these differences could be taken into account by specifying a labial component for the vowel which has lip compression, as opposed to rounding (which implies lip protrusion) for the other vowels in table 49.

Table 49 Contrasts involving high rounded vowels in Swedish. The vowel in this language is said to have lip compression as opposed to lip rounding as in the other vowels illustrated.

| v y : | view | h ʉ : s | house | s ø : t | sweet |
| s y : n | sight | n ʉ : | now | r ø : d | red |

Tension is also a binary opposition at the systematic phonemic level. Even at the phonetic level it seems that we do not need to specify degrees of this feature; but this may be simply because our phonetic specifications of vowels are still so inadequate. Examples of contrasting tense and lax vowels in Igbirra are given in table 50.

Table 50 Contrasts between tense and lax vowels in Igbirra. Note that because of the vowel harmony restrictions in the language the first person pronoun prefix is mé- before tense vowels and má- before lax vowels.

Tense		Lax	
mézɪ̀	I expect	mázɪ̀	I am in pain
mézɛ́	I am well	mázɛ̀	I agree
métɔ́	I arrange	mátɔ́	I pick
métʊ́	I beat	mátʊ́	I send

The most appropriate way of summarizing this discussion of the features of vowel quality is by reference to the array of symbols shown in figure 13. The tense-lax opposition has been left out of this figure because there is no generally agreed arrangement of symbols for tense and lax vowels which does not conflate some of the different degrees of height represented in figure 13. A common way of symbolizing tense and lax vowels was illustrated in table 50; and if a distinction between low, central or front, tense and lax vowels is required, the symbols a and æ may be used. There seems to be no need for a way of specifying this opposition among front rounded, central, or back unrounded vowels.

As figure 13 indicates, in front rounded and back unrounded vowels, only two degrees of vowel height need be recognized at the systematic phonemic level; the symbol œ is given in parentheses since many languages (e.g., French and Danish) require three degrees at the systematic phonetic level. For the central vowels, two degrees of lip rounding are needed only for the high vowels.

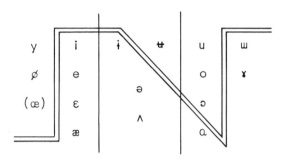

Fig. 13. Three of the features of vowel quality. HEIGHT is represented on the vertical axis; BACKNESS on the horizontal axis; and ROUND vowels are above the double line.

Even with these restrictions the figure shows more possibilities within a feature than I have observed. Thus I do not know of any use of the three central unrounded vowels ɨ ə ʌ within one language; and I doubt that there are examples of contrasts between the three unrounded mid vowels e ə ɤ .

Before leaving the subject of vowels we must conclude the discussion of the secondary articulations, palatalization, velarization, and pharyngealization, which we postponed at the end of the preceding chapter. We must also consider the relation between the terms front, central, and back, which we have been using as the set of possibilities within the backness feature, and the terms postalveolar, palatal, velar, uvular, and pharyngeal, which we had defined as being among the members of the set of possible places of articulation. At first sight it might seem appropriate to consider back to be equivalent to velar, and front to be equivalent to postalveolar or palatal (and we have already noticed that it may not be necessary to distinguish between these two possibilities when the tip of the tongue is not involved). But we do not achieve a satisfactory solution by completely collapsing the backness feature within the articulatory place feature in this way. In the first place, it is plainly wrong to consider low back vowels to be velar sounds. Second, if we do not have separate, additional, features for vowels, we cannot consider consonants with secondary articulations to have added vowellike characteristics. In the feature system being proposed here vowels will be assigned a value both for the backness and height features and also for the articulatory place feature; and consonants will also have values for backness as well as place. Some illustrations are given in table 51. Specifications of this kind allow us to write natural assimilation rules in which, for example, the lowering and backing of a vowel before a pharyngeal consonant, or the palatalization of a velar consonant before a front vowel, are both expressed as a change of the features of one segment so that they become more like those of the adjacent segment.

Table 51 Example of feature assignments for some vowels and some consonants with and without secondary articulations. (Note: the IPA does not distinguish between a velarized consonant z^{w} and a pharyngealized consonant $z^{ˤ}$; both would be written ẓ .)

	i c	u k	kʲ	l	ɤ	ħ a	$z^{ˤ}$ (=IPA ẓ)
Articulatory place	palatal	velar	velar	alveolar	alveolar	pharyngeal	alveolar
Backness	front	back	front	central	back	back	back
Height	high	high	high	high	high	low	low

9.   Prosodic Features

So far we have discussed features for specifying both vowels and consonants; but we have not considered criteria for distinguishing between these two classes. We have not, for instance, discussed the relation between vowels and the class of consonants we called approximants, other than to suggest that they may differ in terms of the rate feature. There are, in particular, the so-called semivowels   j w ɥ   , which are very similar to the corresponding vowels   i u y   (see tables 36 and 45 for examples of all these sounds in French); and it does not seem possible to distinguish between these two groups of sounds simply in terms of the rate of change of articulatory position. On some occasions semivowels have a steady-state portion which is comparatively long (Lehiste 1964), and may be longer than that in some vowels. A better solution (basically that of Pike 1943) is to distinguish between vowels and semivowels by calling the one group syllabic approximants, and the other nonsyllabic approximants. We shall at any rate need to distinguish between syllabic and nonsyllabic sounds in other cases, such as the   l   sounds in *coddling* and *codling*; in my speech these words differ by having an identical number of segments (there is no extra vowel in the first word) with identical properties, except for the syllabicity of the   l . (It is, of course, irrelevant that at some level of phonological abstraction there might be an extra vowel represented in the first word; the final phonetic representation must be able to characterize the difference in the way described above.)

We will therefore posit a feature SYLLABIC; but it must be admitted that there are great difficulties in defining it. There are no directly observable physiological or acoustic properties clearly distinguishing syllabic and non-syllabic segments. But perhaps this is being overly simplistic in our view of physiological properties. Although there is no single muscular gesture marking each syllable (Ladefoged 1958, 1967), we may still be able to define a physiological unit of this kind which will account for the timing and coordination of the articulatory movements. There is evidence (Kozhevnikov and Chistovich 1965; Ladefoged 1967; Lindblom 1968) that speakers organize the sequences of complex muscular events that make up utterances in terms of a hierarchy of units, one of which is of the size of a syllable; and it is certainly true that speakers usually know how many syllables there are in an utterance. We will therefore assume that a neurophysiological definition is possible, even if we cannot at the moment state it in any way.

Syllabic sounds are usually longer than nonsyllabic sounds. But in addition many languages use contrasts in the lengths of segments which are not simply due to one sound being syllabic and the other not. We have already seen that we need a feature rate of articulation, which could be used to specify these variations; but in the earlier discussion we did not consider examples of segmental contrasts. Rate of articulation is, of course, a relative quality, much influenced by rate of utterance (which itself may be partially determined by the age and emotional state of the speaker).

Comparatively few languages use contrasts between long and short consonants within the same morpheme; Italian is a well-known example (see table 52). But many languages have contrasting long and short vowels. In some Bantu languages vowel length may be used to mark not only lexical oppositions but also other grammatical contrasts. This leads to there being possibly four degrees of vowel length in Kamba. I do not know of any four-way contrasts at the systematic phonetic level, but sets of three occur as shown in table 53.

The situation is further complicated by the fact that variations in stress also affect the length of sounds. As we say in chapter 3, sounds which differ in stress differ in the amount of respiratory work done and in laryngeal activity.

Table 52 Contrasts involving long and short consonants in Italian

fato	fate	fat:o	done	kade	he falls	kad:e	he fell
fola	fable	fol:a	crowd	nono	ninth	non:o	grandfather

Table 53 Contrasts in vowel length in Kamba (suggested by Wilfred Whiteley; cf. Whiteley and Muli 1962). The four degrees of length are represented as: a   a·   a: a::

kwele la	measuring	koʃa	start
kwele·la	moving backward and forward		
koele:la	aiming at	koʃa:	giving birth
		koʃa::	giving birth frequently

82

The extra respiratory work usually results in greater length, as well as increases in pitch and loudness. Lieberman (1960) and Lindblom (1968) have shown how variations in duration, fundamental frequency, and intensity (the acoustic counterparts of length, pitch, and loudness) can be correlated with variations in stress patterns.

Definitions of the feature STRESS are difficult to formalize. A possible starting point is provided by Öhman (1967, p. 47), who considers stress to be "the addition of a quantum of physiological energy to the speech production system as a whole . . . distributed (possibly unevenly) over the pulmonary, phonatory, and articulatory channels." Recent work by Netsell (1970) has done much to justify this view. But Netsell's results indicate that increased articulatory energy is the least important, only occurring spasmodically in very heavy stresses. His work also shows that people differ in the degree to which they use laryngeal as opposed to respiratory activity. At the moment we do not know how to sum up physiological energy which has been distributed over different components of the speech system. There is no way of equating the consumption of respiratory energy with the degree of activity of the laryngeal muscles. Consequently we may have to regard stress as being an auditory quality with incompletely defined physiological characteristics.

There is, however, another function of the phonetic entity stress which may lead us to consider it is something that either does or does not occur. Like syllabicity, stress is an organizing principle. In many languages the timing of utterances is organized at least partly in terms of stress groups. As has been shown by Allen (1971) syllables and stresses are the only units involved in the rhythm of English phrases. Similar observations have been made by Kozhevnikov and Chistovich (1965) for Russian. In this sense a stress group either occurs or it does not occur; there do not seem to be major stress groups and minor stress groups. In order to organize the timing beats in an utterance, a speaker of English requires only one kind of unit larger than the syllable, and smaller than the breath group (a unit which we will discuss subsequently).

This view of stress contrasts with the view presented by Chomsky and Halle (1968, p. 116, fn. 68), who claim that "it is easy to detect at least five degrees of stress in English." We are not, of course, concerned here with the way Chomsky and Halle predict the positions and levels of the stresses within English words from a knowledge of the syntax. As we have already noted, it is irrelevant to setting up a system of features that some of these features are required for specifying syntactic rather than lexical contrasts. The point at issue is simply the number of stress levels which occur in English at the systematic phonetic level.

There is no doubt that English (and many other languages) has two contrasting levels of stress, as illustrated by noun-verb pairs such as *an insult — to insult.* The traditional descriptions of English (Jones 1956; Kenyon and Knott 1953) mark an additional level of stress in that they show some syllables as having primary stress, some as having secondary stress, and others as being unstressed. On the whole, Jones marks secondary stresses as occurring only before primary stresses within a word (as in ˌgˌzæmıˈneʃn) whereas Kenyon and Knott mark them both before and after primary stresses. But it is not at all clear to me that Kneyon and Knott are using the term secondary stress in a single consistent way. Those instances where they mark a secondary stress after a primary stress (as in ˈænɪkˌdot) simply show that the vowel in that syllable is unreduced. Those which they (like Jones) place before a primary stress (as in ˌærəˈstɑkrəsɪ) mark points of potentially greater physiological energy; but they are not necessarily lesser in stress (as I use this term) than the points with a primary stress mark. Of course the first syllable of a word such as *aristocracy* is very different from the third, at least when the word is said in isolation. But this is because the third syllable is then the last stressed syllable in a breath group, and is accompanied by the major pitch change which is the appropriate intonation contour for a one-word sentence. In a sentence such as *The aristocracy suffers* the first and third syllables are either equal in stress (as occurs when this sentence is spoken in a slow formal style with three stress beats) or the first syllable is unstressed but with an unreduced vowel, and only the third syllable is stressed (as occurs when this sentence is said more rapidly with only two stress beats). Consequently, even at the phonetic level, we may need to distinguish between only the two possibilities, stressed and unstressed, plus the possibility of reduced as opposed to unreduced vowels. This latter phenomenon may be best regarded as determined by a degree of the syllabicity feature.

The more we look at prosodic features, the more apparent it is that their physiological correlates are inextricably combined. As is obvious from the preceding paragraphs, the feature stress has a great influence on some of the pitch changes which occur in speech. But equally obviously, we need additional phonological features to account for other pitch changes.

All languages use variations in pitch to convey differences in meaning. Table 54 summarizes and illustrates the principal methods. The first division is into the use of pitch for conveying syntactical information (commonly called intonation) as opposed to lexical information (commonly called tone). Thus English varies the intonation of a sentence or a clause to produce differences such as those between a statement or a question, and Chinese varies the tone to

Table 54 Some linguistic uses of pitch. The pitch of the syllables in each example is indicated by the height of the line with reference to the vertical line on the left, which marks a speaker's normal pitch range.

Intonation	Tone	
English:	Contour tone Chinese:	Register tone Yoruba:
Yes		
⌐ I agree (statement)	⌐ ma mother	⌐ o wa he comes
⌐ Did you say "yes"? (question)	⌐ ma hemp	⌐ o wa he looked
⌐ I am listening (continue)	⌐ ma horse	⌐ o wa he exists
⌐ Possibly yes (doubtful)	⌐ ma scold	
⌐ Definitely yes (emphatic)		

produce different lexical meanings. Pike (1948) has suggested a division into contour tone languages such as Chinese, in which the various tones include some in which the essential feature is a changing pitch, as opposed to register tone languages, such as most African languages, where the tones marking the lexical items are comparatively steady state.

In a register tone language such as Yoruba, which has only three discrete levels of tone that contrast at the systematic phonemic level (as shown in table 54), there may be a greater number of observable levels in an utterance because of the action of phonological rules. Thus in Yoruba there is a rule which makes the pitch of each high tone in a sentence slightly lower than the preceding high tone whenever there is an intervening low tone. The result of this rule is to produce a continuous series of downsteps, giving a terraced-level effect (cf. Welmers 1959) whereby the pitches of the high tones in a sentence get progressively lower as the sentence goes on. In Twi the same kind of rule applies even after a high tone which exists in the underlying form, but which is not present in an actual utterance, because of the elision of a vowel. Thus in the Twi example in table 55 (based on Schachter 1961) the stem of the word meaning *fire* has a high pitch when it occurs as the first high tone after a low pitch (as it does when it has only a nominal prefix); but it is one step lower when it is the second high tone and occurs with an intervening (elided) low tone, as it does when preceded by the name *Kofi*; and it is one step lower still when it occurs after a tone which is itself a step down from the highest possible pitch, as in the third syllable of the name *Akua*.

Table 55 Examples (suggested by Paul Schachter) of the downstep effect in Twi

⎡ ‾		⎡ ‾ ‾		⎡ ‾‾ ‾	
⎣ō ɟa	a fire	⎣k̄of i ɟa	Kofi's fire	⎣ā kua ɟa	Akua's fire

Downstep phenomena clearly indicate that any feature system for describing tonal phenomena must be capable of a multivalued interpretation at the systematic phonetic level. But it does not, of course, follow that multivalued tonal features are appropriate at the classificatory level. This would be true only if languages had phonological rules which required that there be a similar relationship between each (phonemic) tone and the tone with the next highest pitch.

In an excellent article on the phonological features required in the description of tone languages, Wang (1967) has convincingly argued that binary tonal features are required to account for many of the phenomena that need explanation within phonological rules. But as Wang himself says in the same article, "a phonological theory must be able to provide alternative feature representations for the same sounds." Consequently we must not assume that multivalued features are always inappropriate just because binary features are required for the efficient operation of some phonological rules. That one sometimes wants to separate out, say, a mid tone and oppose it to both high and low tones does not preclude the possibility that at other times one might want to regard high, mid, and low tones as members of a linearly ordered set. Thus it seems that the tone-lowering phenomena which Wang (1967) describes as occurring in Gaoxiong may be more appropriately stated in terms of a multivalued tonal feature, using phonological conventions similar to those used by Chomsky and Halle (1968) in their description of stress lowering in English.

Apart from the question whether a multivalued feature of tone height is needed, for the purposes of this book we can clearly do no better than to use Wang's features for categorizing tonal phenomena. Table 56 shows how Wang uses his seven features to specify thirteen tones. The top line shows the phonetic characteristics of each of these tones using the "tone letter" notation proposed by Chao (1924). The dashed line encloses a minimum specification of these tones, the values for the other features being supplied by a set of redundancy rules which Wang gives. Wang notes that there are probably no languages with more than five tone levels.

Table 56 Tones and their features (from Wang 1967)

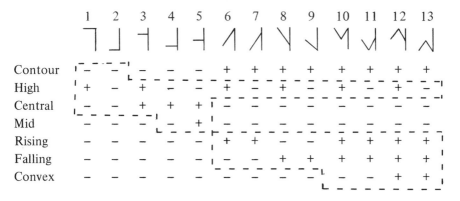

	1	2	3	4	5	6	7	8	9	10	11	12	13
Contour	−	−	−	−	−	+	+	+	+	+	+	+	+
High	+	−	+	−	−	+	−	+	−	+	−	+	−
Central	−	−	+	+	+	−	−	−	−	−	−	−	−
Mid	−	−	−	−	+	−	−	−	−	−	−	−	−
Rising	−	−	−	−	−	+	+	−	−	+	+	+	+
Falling	−	−	−	−	−	−	−	+	+	+	+	+	+
Convex	−	−	−	−	−	−	−	−	−	−	−	+	+

The distinction between tone languages and intonation languages is not as precise as might be imagined from the preceding paragraphs. In practice most tone languages always have a mixture of methods of using pitch (cf. Gleason 1961). There is probably no language, however tonal, which does not have some intonation features corresponding to a grammatical unit such as a clause or a sentence. As is shown in table 57, there are (1) tone languages like Yoruba which have some form of lowering of the final tone; and (2) other tone languages like Hausa which have a falling or a rising intonation pattern over the whole sentence. It should be noted that final lowering is quite a different phenomenon from the downstep or terraced-level effects discussed above. It is quite possible to have a sentence in Yoruba in which the sequence of tones is

Table 57 Combinations of tonal and intonational features

1. Tone on all items, intonation in parts of some utterances; e.g., "final lowering" in Yoruba

2. Tone on all items, intonation throughout; e.g., "downdrift" in Hausa (example suggested by David Arnott):

maIam insu yana ba su nama
'teacher their he gives them meat'

note also question:

maIam insu yana ba su nama

3. Tone on some items, intonation throughout; e.g., Fula (example suggested by David Arnott):

o waddii ceede den hande   o waddii ceede fun hande
'he's brought money the today'   'he's brought money all today'

4. No tone, intonation throughout; e.g., English

such that there will be no downsteps; but the syntactically caused final lowering will still be present. In addition to all these effects, which involve the superimposition of intonation on tone languages, there are also the reverse kind of phenomena. Thus there are (3) some languages which are usually classified as nontonal but nevertheless have some words which have characteristic pitches. Fula may be taken as an example of such a language, in that it does not use lexical pitch variations except in a small set of words which always have a high tone, and which cause a disturbance in the intonation pattern whenever they occur. Finally (4) there are languages, such as English, in which (if we exclude the effects of stress) no word has a predetermined pitch pattern.

There have been very few attempts at setting up a comprehensive set of features suitable for the description of intonation languages. Lieberman (1967) proposed that English could be described in terms of the oppositions ±prominence, which corresponds to our feature accent, and ±breath group, which entails the presence or absence of laryngeal activity of the kind which produces a rise in pitch. These features are obviously not sufficient to account for all the phenomena that occur.

A better set of features for characterizing intonation in a language like English has been suggested by Vanderslice (1968). For the set of features to be proposed here we will follow him and distinguish between CADENCE and ENDGLIDE. Cadence refers to the presence or absence of a fall in pitch or a particular syllable, and endglide refers to the presence or absence of a rise in pitch after that syllable and continuing for the remainder of the breath group. These two features can be combined as shown in table 58 so that they discriminate between four possibilities. Vanderslice is careful to point out that these two features are far from sufficient to account for all the patterns that occur in an intonation language. He suggests that we will also need ±pause (a terminal drawl), and ±emphasis (extra pitch raising), as well as features to describe the variations in tessitura or characteristic pitch range which occur when quoting or attributing one utterance within another, and additional features to describe dipped and scooped pitch changes (cf. Bolinger 1965). There is no doubt that some extra features are needed, but it is not clear to me which of these are within the scope of this book in that they specify linguistically contrasting patterns and which ones are required only for paralinguistic phenomena.

Table 58   The use of the features cadence and endglide for the specification of some basic intonation patterns (after Vanderslice 1968)

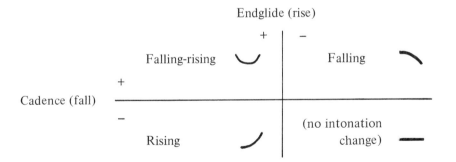

10.   Feature Systems

The complete set of features which we have been discussing is listed in table 59. This table shows the name given to each feature, the maximum number of contrasts which have been observed at the systematic phonemic level, and a largely arbitrary number of terms which can be used to describe values of the feature at the systematic phonetic level. Note that there is one extra feature, CONSONANTAL, which has not been mentioned previously. This feature has a different status from all other features in that it can be defined only in terms of the intersection of classes already defined by other features. Thus nonconsonantal sounds are nonlateral and sonorant. They correspond largely to what Pike (1943) called vocoids, which he defined as central, resonant orals. We will return to this point at the end of this chapter.

Note that, without including the tone features, twenty features are used as binary oppositions at the systematic phonemic level. Of the remaining six features, two (glottalicness and rate) are either binary or not used at all in all but a handful of languages; and two others (glottal stricture and voice onset) are used as binary oppositions in the majority of languages. There seems to be no doubt that as Jakobson (1962) has repeatedly pointed out, the binary principle is a major factor in human communication.

There are, however, two features which nearly all languages use in a nonbinary way. The first of these is the articulatory place feature. With the exception of labials and velars, which are linked by the auditory feature gravity, there seems to be little motivation for combining places of articulation in any particular way. It may be that in some languages which have more than three places of articulation there are rules which constantly refer to, say, the front pair as opposed to the back pair. If this is so, we might have to add the feature front. But even if this feature is needed it is not clear to me whether it should be said to have its own phonetic properties, or whether it should be defined simply in terms of existing features. Smith (1971) has suggested the additional possibility of a feature encompassing all sounds in which the tip or blade of the tongue is involved. This might enlarge our system for describing places of articulation in a very useful way.

I suggested earlier (p. 43) that the different places might be regarded as independent items (all phonologically equidistant from one another) within one multivalued feature. Alternatively, each place of opposition could be regarded as a separate binary feature (bilabial–nonbilabial, dental–nondental, etc.) operating within a convention that states that a plus value for any one of these features implies a minus value for all the others. This would allow one to

91

Table 59 Summary of the proposed feature system

	Name of feature	Maximum number of systematic phenemic contrasts	Arbitrarily specified terms for use at systematic phonetic level
0.	Consonantal	2	(not applicable at the phonetic level)
1.	Glottal stricture	3	glottal stop creak creaky voice tense (stiff) voice voice lax (slack) voice murmur breathy voice voiceless
2.	Voice onset	3	voicing throughout articulation voicing during part of articulation voicing starts immediately after voicing starts shortly after voicing starts considerably later
3.	Fortis–lenis	2	normal respiratory activity heightened subglottal pressure
4.	Glottalicness	3	ejective (glottis moving air upward) pulmonic implosive (glottis moving air downward)
5.	Velaric suction	2	no click click (ingressive velaric airstream)
6.	Nasality	(2)	oral (velic closure) nasal (velic opening)
7.	Prenasality	2	not prenasalized prenasalized
8.	Articulatory place	6	bilabial labiodental dental alveolar postalveolar palatal velar uvular pharyngeal glottal labial-velar labial-alveolar

Table 59 Summary of the proposed feature system (continued)

9.	Gravity	2	higher pitch spectral energy lower pitch spectral energy
10.	Apicality	2	tip of tongue blade of tongue
11.	Stop	2	no complete articulatory closure stop closure
12.	Fricative	2	no turbulence maximum turbulence
13.	Vibration	2	no vibration vibration (trilled)
14.	Rate	(3)	rapid normal long extra long
15.	Laterality	2	central lateral
16.	Sibilance	2	no high pitch turbulence high pitch turbulence
17.	Sonorant	2	less intensity in the formants greater acoustic energy in the formants
18.	Rounding	2	lips spread lips neutral lips closely rounded
19.	Height	4	low mid-low mid-high high
20.	Backness	(2)	no tongue retraction body of tongue retracted
21.	Tension	2	tongue hollowed no intrinsic tongue contaction tongue bunched

Table 59 Summary of the proposed feature system (continued)

22.	Syllabicity	2	nonsyllabic
			syllabic (correlates undefined)
23.	Accent	(2)	not stressed
			maximal stress pulse
24.	Tone (as in Wang 1967)		contour
			high
			central
			mid
			rising
			falling
			convex
25.	Cadence	2	no intonation change
			falling intonation
26.	Endglide	2	no intonation change
			final rising intonation

remain within a theory which permits only binary oppositions at the classificatory level. But it is not clear to me why such importance should be attached to this constraint, since it is obvious that all phonological theories must be able to formalize rules containing nonbinary features. Multivalued features are used in nearly a third of the rule schemata suggested by Chomsky and Halle (1968) for describing the phonology of English.

The second feature which is nonbinary in nearly all languages is vowel height. In this instance there are clear grounds for claiming that this is a scalar feature, in which even at the systematic phonemic level some items (mid vowels) are regarded as being potentially between others (high and low vowels). This claim will be mentioned again in reviewing alternative feature systems in this chapter.

A useful way of reviewing and exemplifying the feature system proposed in this book is to compare it with that proposed by Chomsky and Halle (1968) in the chapter entitled "The Phonetic Framework" in *The sound pattern of English*. We will not be concerned here with the theoretical issues raised there.

For our present purposes it does not matter whether there are contradictions between their statements (all with my italics) such as:

> all grammatically determined facts about the *production* and *perception* . . . are embodied in the "phonetic transcription." [p. 293]

> phonetic transcription is . . . a representation of what the speaker of a language *takes to be* the phonetic properties of an utterance . . . . physically identical signals may have distinct phonetic transcriptions. [p. 294]

> the phonetic representation can be thought of formally as a two-dimensional matrix in which the columns stand for consecutive units and the rows stand for individual phonetic features. The phonetic features can be characterized as *physical scales*, describing independently controllable aspects of the speech event . . . . [p. 297]

I have examined some of these issues elsewhere (Ladefoged 1971a, 1971b), and for the moment will restrict the discussion to the ways in which the particular linguistic contrasts would be represented in the different feature systems.

We may begin by considering the Chomsky-Halle treatment of differences in phonation type. They use four binary features for this purpose: voiced–nonvoiced (voiceless), glottal constriction, heightened subglottal pressure, and tense–nontense (lax). Their use of the terms voiced and voiceless is essentially the same as ours in chapter 2, and needs no further comment. But a few remarks are needed on each of the other features.

Chomsky and Halle are not very precise in their definition of glottal constriction, saying (p. 315): "Glottal constrictions are formed by narrowing the glottal aperture beyond its neutral position." Their subsequent discussion indicates that they would probably specify positive values of this feature for several of the lower values of our feature glottal stricture, namely those corresponding to tense voice, laryngealization (creaky voice and creak), and glottal stop.

The Chomsky-Halle feature heightened subglottal pressure is obviously very similar to the feature we called fortis; but they use this feature in a slightly different way. We saw earlier (p. 24) that some consonants, such as the fortis stops in Korean, the strong consonants in Luganda, and the fortis nasals in Kachin-Jingpho may be produced with heightened subglottal pressure. But

95

Chomsky and Halle seem to believe that many other consonants have positive values of this feature. They say (p. 326), "Heightened subglottal pressure is a necessary but not sufficient condition for aspiration. Aspiration requires, in addition, that there be no constriction at the glottis." This implies that the voiceless initial stops in English, which are clearly aspirated, have a heightened subglottal pressure. Not only is there no evidence in favor of this notion, but also there is plenty of published data (e.g., Ladefoged 1967, pp. 41-44; Lieberman 1967, p. 77) showing that it is untrue. More recently, Netsell (1969), in a study explicitly directed to the investigation of subglottal pressure during English t and d , found that "the respiratory system generates an essentially invariant driving pressure" for these two sounds.

Chomsky and Halle require the feature heightened subglottal pressure in their description of the murmured stops (voiced aspirated stops, in their terminology) which occur in Hindi. My own experimental observations on similar languages (and those of John Ohala on Hindi, personal communication) cannot be interpreted unambiguously. There is sometimes, but not always, an increase in the subglottal pressure toward the end of murmured stops. This might be due to an "independently controllable aspect of the speech event" as Chomsky and Halle require for their features. But it might be simply a result of variations in the state of the glottis, and not independently controllable in any way.

Finally, in this group we must consider the use Chomsky and Halle make of the feature tense—nontense (lax). They restrict this feature entirely to supraglottal articulations, and do not consider it to be associated with tensing of the vocal cords in any way. But it has a bearing on the present discussion of phonation types because they consider the walls of the pharynx to be necessarily lax in voiced stops. They claim that it is this laxing which permits the enlargement of the vocal tract which is required during voiced stops; if the oral cavity did not become larger, air could not continue to flow through the glottis and maintain vibrations of the vocal cords. The enlargement of the pharynx during voiced stops is a well-known phenomenon. But most investigators now believe that this enlargement is not due to the increase in oral pressure resulting in the lax walls of the pharynx being pushed back; nor is it generally held that in voiceless stops there is no such enlargement because the tense walls of the pharynx actively resist it. Chomsky and Halle base their conclusions on data for four utterances, one each of t d s z by a single subject, reported by Perkell (1965; see also the later monograph, Perkell 1969, for additional analysis of the same data). But the indirect observations by Lisker and Abramson (1967) combined with later cineradiographic studies by

Kent and Moll (1969) and electromyographic studies by Smith (personal communication) point to different conclusions. The enlargement of the vocal tract during voiced stops is an active muscular process, and there is no increase in the tension of the pharyngeal muscles during voiceless stops.

Table 60 shows the way Chomsky and Halle would presumably specify some of the sounds described earlier in this book, using the features discussed above. The specification in terms of the features we have been considering is also given. It is clear that the Chomsky-Halle system is sufficiently rich for them to be able to specify any of these sounds unambiguously. But, as we have seen in the preceding paragraphs, there is sometimes very little supporting phonetic evidence for their features; and as our knowledge of the rules that operate in these languages is very slight, there is also very little phonological evidence in favor of the Chomsky-Halle features.

Table 60 The specification of some sounds which differ in their phonation types by means of the Chomsky-Halle features in comparison with those suggested here. Note that the numbers shown in the latter system designate simply the classificatory contrasts and their relative positions on the scale. They do not show the values at the systematic phonetic level which depend on the action of phonological rules.

	*p	pʰ	p	b̤	b	b̰	
	−	−	−	+	+	+	Voicing
	+	+	−	−	−	+	Tense
	+	−	−	−	−	+	Glottal constriction
Chomsky and Halle	+	+	−	+	−	−	Heightened subglottal pressure
Ladefoged							
Margi (table 7)			0		1	2	Glottal stricture
Sindhi (table 14)		0	0	1	2		Glottal stricture
		2	1	2	0		Voice onset
Korean (table 12)	1	0	0				Glottal stricture
	0	1	0				Voice onset
	1	1	0				Fortis

The alternative set of features given here is, of course, multivalued. The values given in the table are those for the features considered as classificatory devices. They indicate simply the number of contrasts which occur at the classificatory level and their relative places on the scale. The set of phonological rules (in particular the lower-level rules) assigns the appropriate values for the systematic phonetic level.

One of the major differences between the two systems is the way they treat cases of what might be called the same sound in different languages (or, to be more accurate, sounds which are symbolized by the same letter in different languages). Thus, in the particular set of sounds shown in table 60, the b in Margi is given the same feature specification as the b in Hindi in the Chomsky-Halle system. But in the system proposed here, they are given different specifications because, in the case of Margi, it is important for the phonological rules to show that b is between b̰ and p ; whereas in Hindi b is the extreme value of the glottal stricture feature, and b̤ is between it and p . The use of a multivalued system allows the sound patterns which occur to be described in terms of a more explanatory set of rules.

It is quite appropriate for a segment which seems to be the same in two different languages to be nevertheless given a different specification at the sytematic phonemic level in these two languages. If the sounds in the different languages are pronounced in the same way, then the phonological rules must ensure that they will have the same representation at the systematic phonetic level. Thus one level of representation will allow us to compare and contrast phonological systems in different languages, and the other will allow us to compare and contrast the actual sounds. Chomsky and Halle would also show a difference in the systematic phonemic representations of Margi b and Sindhi b if each of these sounds operated in a different way in the phonologies of the two languages.

The issue of whether classificatory features should be binary (as proposed by Chomsky-Halle) or multivalued (as proposed here) is not in itself very relevant to a choice between feature systems. Any multivalued feature can be reinterpreted in terms of a number of binary features; and any binary system can be supplied with marking conventions so that it acts as if it contained multivalued features. What is far more relevant to a comparison is the difference in the claims that each system makes both about the phonological relations between sounds and about the phonetic facts.

There are potentially four binary features in the Chomsky-Halle system which can be used for specifying sounds made with a supplementary airstream mechanism: velaric pressure, velaric suction (click), glottalic pressure (ejection), and glottalic suction (implosion). Chomsky and Halle note that no language uses the first of these possibilities. Their use of the other three features is comparable to our use of the features velaric suction and glottalicness. With regard to the latter feature, there is obviously very little difference between a multivalued feature system with the three possibilities corresponding to ejective, plosive, and implosive and a binary system which uses two features ±glottalic pressure and ±glottalic suction, together with a convention that prohibits the co-occurrence of plus values for both features. Examples of the use of both systems are given in table 61.

Table 61 The specification of sounds differing in their airstream mechanisms.

		Zulu (table 16)			
	Uduk (table 15)				
	ɗ	t '	t	ɬ	
	–	–	–	+	Velaric suction
	+	–	–	–	Glottalic suction
Chomsky and Halle	–	+	–	–	Glottalic pressure
Ladefoged	0	0	0	1	Velaric suction
	–1	+1	0	0	Glottalicness

There may be an additional complication in the specification of clicks which we have not considered. Chomsky and Halle base their description of the Hottentot clicks on Beach (1938). This leads them to posit a feature, delayed release of secondary closure, to account for the velar affricate quality which Beach found in some of these clicks. This quality does not occur in the clicks in the Nguni languages discussed on pages 28-29, and I have not had an opportunity to hear it in any of the languages described by Beach. But Beach was obviously a very good phonetic observer, and it may well be that we should include a feature of this kind within our system.

Places of articulation cannot be specified very easily in binary terms. Chomsky and Halle make use of the notion of a "neutral position" of the tongue, which they define as "the level that it occupies in the articulation of the English vowel [e] in the word *bed*" (p. 300). They are also careful to point out that in the neutral position the blade of the tongue is not raised. Data from cineradiography indicate that just before a speaker begins to talk there is a "speech readiness" position. But as far as I know, there is no evidence that this position is the level of that in the vowel [e]. Nor is there any evidence that the tongue tends to go to such a level during the moments in utterances when its action is unspecified.

Chomsky and Halle use seven features to describe variations in place of articulation and some aspects of what we have called secondary articulations. The definitions of these features as given in *The sound pattern of English* are:

CORONAL–NONCORONAL
Coronal sounds are produced with the blade of the tongue raised from its neutral position; noncoronal sounds are produced with the blade of the tongue in the neutral position.

ANTERIOR–NONANTERIOR
Anterior sounds are produced with an obstruction that is located in front of the palato-alveolar region of the mouth; nonanterior sounds are produced without such an obstruction. The palato-alveolar region is that where the ordinary English [š] is produced.

HIGH–NONHIGH
High sounds are produced by raising the body of the tongue above the level that it occupies in the neutral position; nonhigh sounds are produced without such a raising of the tongue body.

LOW–NONLOW
Low sounds are produced by lowering the body of the tongue below the level that it occupies in the neutral position; nonlow sounds are produced without such a lowering of the body of the tongue.

BACK–NONBACK
Back sounds are produced by retracting the body of the tongue from the neutral position; nonback sounds are produced without such a retraction from the neutral position.

ROUNDED–NONROUNDED
Rounded sounds are produced with a narrowing of the lip orifice; nonrounded sounds are produced without such a narrowing.

DISTRIBUTED–NONDISTRIBUTED
Distributed sounds are produced with a constriction that extends for a considerable distance along the direction of the air flow; nondistributed sounds are produced with a constriction that extends only for a short distance in this direction.

The first five of these features can be represented on an articulatory diagram (assuming there are no secondary articulations) as shown in figure 14. The other two features are also fairly straightforward. The Chomsky-Halle feature round is virtually the same as our feature rounding, except that Chomsky and Halle consider it possible to use an extreme degree of their feature in the specification of labial-velars. We thought it preferable to set up an additional term within the articulatory place feature to account for these sounds. Finally, their feature distributed–nondistributed corresponds largely to our feature apicality, and to the bilabial-labiodental opposition in our set of places of articulation.

The relation between the Chomsky-Halle features and the terms within our place of articulation feature and apicality feature is as shown in table 62.

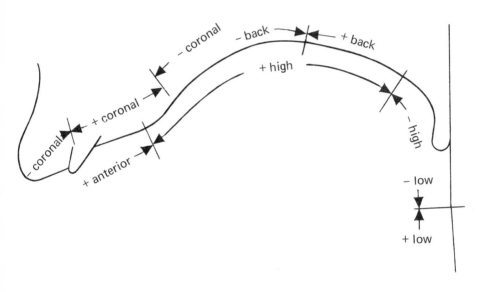

Fig. 14. A representation of the binary features suggested by Chomsky and Halle (1968) in terms of an articulatory diagram.

Table 62 The relation between the terms within the place of articulation feature as used within this book and some Chomsky-Halle features

	Anterior	Coronal	High	Back	Low	Distributed
Bilabial	+	–	–	–	–	+
Labiodental	+	–	–	–	–	–
Dental	+	+	–	–	–	α
Alveolar	+	+	–	–	–	–α
Apical postalveolar (retroflex)	–	+	+	–	–	–
Laminal postalveolar (palatoalveolar)	–	+	+	–	–	+
Palatal	–	–	+	–	–	
Velar	–	–	+	+	–	
Uvular	–	–	–	+	–	
Pharyngeal	–	–	–	+	+	
Glottal	–	–	–	+	+	

Note that Chomsky and Halle can distinguish between dental and alveolar sounds only if one of these has one value of the feature distributed and the other has the opposite value (here denoted α and –α). They claim that no language has dental and alveolar consonants, both with apical articulations. This claim appears to be controverted by the Malayalam data in table 22. It is also impossible for them to consider glottal as a place of articulation distinct from pharyngeal (but they can, of course, consider glottal sounds as distinct in the action of the larynx, using their feature glottal constriction).

The Chomsky-Halle system makes claims about the natural classes which are necessary in phonological descriptions which seem to me to be unfounded. As I argued in chapter 5, it seems preferable to regard the different places of articulation as mutually exclusive terms within a single feature. The only exception is that there clearly is a case for considering some noncoronal sounds as belonging together, as we have recognized by setting up an auditorily defined feature gravity. But note that not all noncoronal sounds fall into this class; pharyngeal sounds are not grave.

Chomsky and Halle use the features discussed above to specify vowels as well as consonants. In the specification of vowels their feature back is exactly the same as our backness feature, except that we allowed for the three terms front, central, and back as possibilities within this feature. There is also a strong resemblance between our feature height and the possible combinations of their two features high and low, which are defined so that the occurrence of +high together with +low is impossible.

There are, however, some very important differences between the two systems in the description of vowels. In the first place the multivalued system shows that there is a relation between possible vowel heights of a kind that cannot be stated in binary terms. It is possible to have a convention that forbids the co-occurrence of +high and +low. But there is no way in which a binary notation can constrain all occurrences of -high, -low (= mid) to be between -high, +low (= low) and +high, -low (= high) in such a way that the change from low to mid involves the same process as the change from mid to high. The notion that there is an ordered relationship between vowel heights is a claim that is made by a multivalued system and not by a binary one. This claim is important in many phonological descriptions of both English (cf. Ladefoged 1967; Foley 1971; Labov 1971) and other languages.

The second difference between the two systems is in the claim made by the Chomsky-Halle system that languages never contrast more than three vowel heights; if there appear to be more than three contrasting heights in a language, Chomsky and Halle would have to say that some other feature (such as tense or round) was involved. I do not know how they would account for the Danish examples given in table 47.

Finally, there are differences in the phonetic claims made by the two system claims that as far as vowels are concerned, languages work partially in auditory terms (the pitch of the first formant, and the distance between the formants being major features of vowel quality) and partially in physiological terms (rounding, tension, and articulatory place must also be taken into account).

It is convenient at this point to consider the use Chomsky and Halle make of their feature tense—nontense in the description of vowels, and to consider another of their features, covered—noncovered, which they also use in the description of vowels. They define this latter feature as follows:
of their feature tense—nontense in the description of vowels, and to consider another of their features, covered—noncovered, which they also use in the description of vowels. They define this latter feature as follows:

We shall assume that covered sounds are produced with a pharynx in which the walls are narrowed and tensed and the larynx raised;

uncovered sounds are produced without a special narrowing and tensing in the pharynx. [p. 315].

Their description of tense sounds is not very explicit. They say:

Tense sounds are produced with a deliberate, accurate, maximally distinct gesture that involves considerable [supraglottal] muscular effort; nontense sounds are produced rapidly and somewhat indistinctly. In tense sounds . . . the period during which the articulatory organs maintain the appropriate configuration is relatively long, while in nontense sounds the entire gesture is executed in a somewhat superficial manner. [p. 324]

They also quote approvingly from Perkell (1965), who says:

the pharynx width remains relatively stable throughout the tense vowels whereas there is a change in this width during the lax vowels . . . . It is as though the tongue shape in the lower pharynx is relatively unconstrained during a lax vowel, and is free to be influenced by the adjacent phonetic segment. For a tense vowel, on the other hand, the tongue position and shape in this region are rather precisely defined. [p. 325]

There is obviously a strong similarity between our feature tongue tension and their features covered—noncovered and tense—nontense. It is probably not profitable to try to resolve the differences at the moment, because (as we noted in chapter 8) we do not have sufficient data concerning the positioning of the tongue in vowels.

We must now consider how Chomsky and Halle explain variations in manner of articulation. The definitions of a number of the features they use are as follows:

NASAL—NONNASAL

Nasal sounds are produced with a lowered velum which allows the air to escape through the nose; nonnasal sounds are produced with a raised velum so that the air from the lungs can escape only through the mouth.

CONTINUANT—NONCONTINUANT (STOP)

In the production of continuant sounds, the primary constriction in the vowel tract is not narrowed to the point where the air flow past the constriction is blocked; in stops the air flow through the mouth is effectively blocked.

DELAYED RELEASE OF PRIMARY CLOSURE – INSTANTANEOUS RELEASE

During the delayed release, turbulence is generated in the vocal tract so that the release phase of affricates is acoustically quite similar to the cognate fricative. The instantaneous release is normally accompanied by much less or no turbulence.

STRIDENT–NONSTRIDENT

Strident sounds are marked acoustically by greater noisiness than their nonstrident counterparts.

LATERAL–NONLATERAL

Lateral sounds are produced by lowering the mid section of the tongue at both sides or at only one side, thereby allowing the air to flow out of the mouth in the vicinity of the molar teeth; in nonlateral sounds no such side passage is open.

The relation between these features and some IPA symbols is as shown in table 63. It will be seen that there are a number of combinations of these features which do not occur. The nasal–nonnasal distinction is possible in continuants, distinguishing, for example, w and w̃ as in the Yoruba examples given in table 17; but as we saw in the discussion at that time (p. 33), neither Yoruba nor any other language that I know of uses a contrast of this kind in its underlying forms. The delayed versus instantaneous release feature obviously applies only to oral stops; and the stridency feature does not apply to nasals or to those oral stops which have an instantaneous release. The laterality feature does not apply to nasals, and probably not to nonstrident stops.

In the feature system proposed in this book we have followed Chomsky and Halle (and the earlier work of Jakobson 1962) in classifying nasals as noncontinuants (stops) as discussed on page 35. Chomsky and Halle note the existence of prenasalized consonants and conclude that "phonetically we have to recognize a feature that governs the timing of movements [of the velum] within the limits of a single segment" (p. 317). This corresponds to our feature prenasality.

The two systems differ considerably in other respects. We have suggested that the two main features for expounding differences in manner of articulation of consonants are stop and fricative. Stops can be either oral or nasal; and if a sound is neither a stop of any kind nor a fricative, it is an approximant. Chomsky and Halle do not have a feature which corresponds

Table 63 Some of the Chomsky-Halle features for explaining variations in the manner of articulation. IPA symbols for the combinations shown are given on the right, assuming that the place of articulation is dental, the glottal stricture and glottal timing that of a voiced sound, there are no supplementary airstream mechanisms, and no secondary articulations.

	Nasal				n
Noncontinuant (stop)	Nonnasal (oral)	Instantaneous release		Central	d
				Lateral	d l
		Delayed release (affricate)	Strident	Central	d z
				Lateral	d ƚ
			Nonstrident		d ð̃
Continuant (nonnasal and with delayed release)			Strident	Central	z
				Lateral	ƚ
			Nonstrident	Central	ð̃
				Lateral	l

directly to our feature fricative. Instead they have a division first into so-called true consonants, a term which we will discuss later, but which for them includes only nasals, stops, and fricatives, and excludes all approximants. Then they specify fricatives as the only true consonants which are +continuant.

Because they do not consider fricative noise a definable attribute of a particular feature, Chomsky and Halle have to specify affricates in some other way. They do so by the addition of a special feature, delayed release of primary closure. The opposition delayed release versus nondelayed release applies only to nonnasal noncontinuants (stops). Given the definitions quoted above it might be thought that all other sounds would be specified as having nondelayed releases; it would hardly make sense to say that l or w or even s was accompanied by turbulence during the release. But, because they do not have fricative as a possible added component, Chomsky and Halle are pushed into the rather ridiculous position of having to have a convention whereby all continuant sounds are regarded as being +delayed release. This is the only way they can arrange for their classification to express correct relationships between stops, affricates, and fricatives, as is shown in table 64. If they had classified continuants as - delayed release, then affricates would have had no relation to fricatives, except perhaps in the stridency feature.

Table 64 The relation between stops, affricates, and fricatives

	∫	t∫	t	
	+	−	−	Continuant
Chomsky and Halle	+	+	−	Delayed release
Ladefoged	0	1	1	Stop
	1	1	0	Fricative

Chomsky and Halle are in even greater difficulties in their specification of trills, taps, and flaps. They claim:

> The distinction between the tap [r] and the trilled [r] is produced by a difference in subglottal pressure: the trilled [r] is produced with heightened subglottal pressure; the tap [r], without it. [p. 318]

As far as I know there is no basis for this claim. They are, however, probably correct in saying:

> it is quite possible that the tongue flap [D] is produced by essentially the same muscular activity that is found in the dental stop articulation, except that in the case of the tongue flap the movement is executed with great rapidity and without tension. [p. 318]

But they leave themselves with a problem, in that they have no feature which specifies rate of movement except perhaps tense−nontense; and they cannot use this feature to specify a contrast between a flap and a regular voiced stop d , since both of them are pronounced without tension. We have the feature articulatory rate making this distinction.

The features discussed in the preceding paragraphs can be used for specifying sounds with different manners of articulation as shown in table 65. Note that even with five features Chomsky and Halle cannot distinguish all these sounds, in that the specification for z and ɾ are the same. Note also

Table 65 The specification of some different manners of articulation in terms of the Chomsky-Halle features and those suggested in this book

	u	w	wˆ	ɽ[=D]	ɾ	r	z	dz	d	
	+	–	–	–	–	–	–	–	–	Vocalic
	–	–	+	+	+	+	+	+	+	Consonantal
	+	+	+	–	+	+	+	–	–	Continuant
	+	+	+	–	+	+	+	+	–	Delayed release
Chomsky and Halle	–	–	–	–	–	+	–	–	–	Heightened subglottal pressure
Ladefoged	0	0	0	1	1	1	0	1	1	Stop
	0	0	1	0	0	0	1	1	0	Fricative
	0	0	0	0	1	1	0	0	0	Vibration
	0	1	1	1	1	0	0	0	0	Rate

that by their present conventions all continuants are +delayed release. It would be a simple matter to change these conventions and make only consonantal continuants (i.e., fricatives and laterals) +delayed release. If this were done vowels and semivowels would be – delayed release, and w would contrast with wˆ in terms of this feature as well as in terms of the consonantality feature. But even for the limited purpose of describing this particular set of sounds it would not be possible to do without the consonantality feature, since the convention would be using it to predict the value of the delayed release feature.

Finally we must consider the features vocalic–nonvocalic, consonantal–nonconsonantal, and sonorant–nonsonorant which Chomsky and Halle use to divide sounds into major classes. We have proposed nothing corresponding to the first of these features. But at the beginning of this chapter we briefly considered a feature consonantal–nonconsonantal. We specified the opposition defined by this feature in terms of classes already established by other features, noting that nonconsonantal sounds are nonlateral sonorants. It might have been easier if we had called this feature vocoid–nonvocoid, and followed Pike (1943) more closely by defining a vocoid as a central, sonorant oral. But by calling the feature consonantal–nonconsonantal (and thus getting forced into the accurate but cumbersome definition in negative terms) we can make the proposed feature system as similar as possible to that suggested by Chomsky and Halle. Their definition of this feature is as follows:

Consonantal sounds are produced with a radical obstruction in the midsagittal region of the vocal tract; nonconsonantal sounds are produced without such an obstruction. [p. 302]

The two definitions differ in that Chomsky and Halle consider glottal sounds such as h and ʕ to be nonconsonantal. But the definitions are alike in that they divide speech sounds into two groups, one containing vowels and glides, and the other including laterals, stops, and fricatives. As we shall see, this results in both feature systems being able to specify some important natural classes of sounds in the same way.

The Chomsky-Halle definition of the feature consonantal–nonconsonantal was not adopted in this book because it seems clear that this feature is unlike others in that it does not have properties which are relevant at the systematic phonetic level. There is not doubt that phonological descriptions of languages will often have to refer to a feature of this kind. But feature systems should be permitted to have a hierarchical structure, so that we allow some features to be defined simply in terms of other features. As our knowledge of the phonological patterns of languages increases it seems likely that we will need additional hierarchical arrangements of this kind.

The Chomsky-Halle feature sonorant differs somewhat from that proposed in this book. Our definition was in terms of an auditory property corresponding to a large amount of acoustic energy within a clearly defined formant structure. This definition is based on the older definition by Jakobson, Fant, and Halle (1952).

Chomsky and Halle (1968) give a physiological description of their features. They say:

Sonorants are sounds produced with a vocal tract cavity configuration in which spontaneous voicing is possible; obstruents are produced with a cavity configuration which makes spontaneous voicing impossible. [p. 302]

Note that this definition is simply in terms of vocal tract shapes; Chomsky and Halle do not require that a sonorant be voiced. Our definition makes voicing a prerequisite for sonorants, since it is the only way to produce a comparatively high acoustic intensity within a well-defined formant structure. But Chomsky and Halle's physiologically based definition leads to glottal stops and voiceless vowels being classified as sonorants, which is counterintuitive to say the least.

We have commented previously that there is no point in trying to define every feature in physiological terms, since the rules of languages are often based on auditory properties of sounds. Furthermore, experimental phoneticians are not at all clear that there are two kinds of voicing: spontaneous voicing which occurs when the vocal tract is unconstricted, and nonspontaneous voicing in which the vocal cords are in a special position so that they can continue to vibrate during stops and fricatives. Chomsky and Halle cite three kinds of experimental evidence for this distinction. First they claim that "the air flow in voiced obstruents is noticeably faster than that in sonorants (vowels, glides, liquids, nasals)" (p. 301). From this they infer that the average glottal opening in voiced obstruents must be greater than that in vowels, and that voiced obstruents must be made with a special adjustment of the larynx. But the data of Klatt, Stevens, and Mead (1968) indicate that the airflow increases in the voiced sibilants z and ʒ , but in other voiced obstruents such as v and ð it is substantially the same as in nasals. I do not know the basis for Chomsky and Halle's claim that the airflow is greater in all voiced obstruents. Second, Chomsky and Halle say that "studies now in progress indicate that at least in the production of some voiced obstruents, the glottis is partially open during the phonation period" (p. 301). Again, there is little evidence that this happens in all voiced obstruents. Third, they suggest that "the very common lengthening of vowels before voiced obstruents can be explained on the grounds that it requires time to shift from the glottis configuration appropriate for vowels to that appropriate for obstruents." As Chen (1970) has shown, this seems an unlikely explanation. The lengthening of vowels before voiced obstruents must be related to the fact that the articulatory gestures of the tongue or lips occur later for these sounds, rather than to supposed niceties of laryngeal adjustment.

In summary, explanations of the feature sonorant in terms of a difference between spontaneous and nonspontaneous voicing seem cumbersome and unmotivated. There is no doubt that we need a feature like sonorant in phonological descriptions. But it should obviously be defined in auditory rather than physiological terms.

Chomsky and Halle suggest in a later chapter (p. 354) that the feature vocalic–nonvocalic might be replaced by a feature syllabic–nonsyllabic. They do not offer a definition of this feature (and it will be remembered that only a few vague remarks have been offered in this book); but if we consider their feature set in this modified form, there is a further increase in the similarity between their system and that proposed here. Table 66 shows how both systems specify the major classes of sounds that are required in phonological descriptions. The specifications given are somewhat redundant. Thus the class of vowels plus glides could be specified simply as the class of - consonantal sounds, there being a convention which automatically makes these sounds +sonorant. The same convention permits vowels to be specified simply as - consonantal +syllabic. Similarly, the class of obstruent consonants (plosives plus fricatives) and the class of consonantal sonorants (nasals plus liquids) need

Table 66 The specification of a number of major natural classes in terms of the two systems

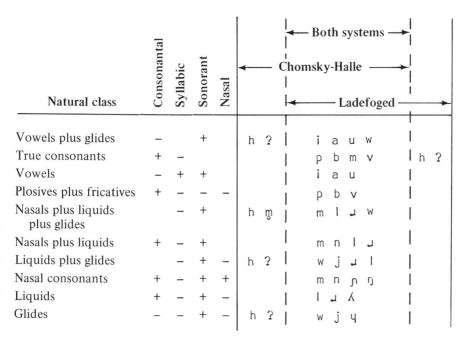

Natural class	Consonantal	Syllabic	Sonorant	Nasal	Both systems / Chomsky-Halle / Ladefoged		
Vowels plus glides	−		+		h ʔ	i a u w	
True consonants	+	−				p b m v	h ʔ
Vowels	−	+	+			i a u	
Plosives plus fricatives	+	−	−	−		p b v	
Nasals plus liquids plus glides		−	+		h m̥	m l ɹ w	
Nasals plus liquids	+	−	+			m n l ɹ	
Liquids plus glides		−	+	−	h ʔ	w j ɹ l	
Nasal consonants	+	−	+	+		m n ɲ ŋ	
Liquids	+	−	+	−		l ɹ ʎ	
Glides	−	−	+	−	h ʔ	w j ɥ	

not be marked −syllabic; nor need nasals be marked as +sonorant. All these values (and a number of others) could be filled in by conventions.

The only major difference between the two systems is in their treatment of the sounds h and ʔ . These sounds are included among the true consonants in our system, whereas Chomsky and Halle consider them to be among the glides. In addition, our system would exclude voiceless nasals from the class of nonsyllabic sonorants, whereas Chomsky and Halle would include them.

The similarity between the two systems is not coincidence. Obviously the feature system proposed in this book (and, in fact, the whole idea of the importance of phonological features in the description of languages) owes a great deal to the earlier work of Jakobson, and its development by Chomsky and Halle. But, as many sections of this book have shown, the state of our ignorance is such that we have to find better answers to many phonetic problems before we can take full advantage of their theoretical insights.

Bibliography

Abercrombie, David. 1967. *Elements of general phonetics*. Chicago: Aldine.

Allen, George. 1971. The location of rhythmic stress beats in English: An experimental study. *Language and Speech*. In press.

Beach, D. M. 1938. *The phonetics of the Hottentot language*. Cambridge: Heffer.

Bolinger, Dwight. 1965. *Forms of English*. Cambridge: Harvard University Press.

Catford, John C. 1964. Phonation types: The classification of some laryngeal components of speech production. In *In honour of Daniel Jones*, edited by David Abercrombie, D. B. Fry, P. A. D. MacCarthy, N. C. Scott, and J. L. M. Trim, pp. 26-37. London: Longmans.

———— 1968. The articulatory possibilities of man. In *Manual of phonetics*, edited by Bertil Malmberg, pp. 309-33. Amsterdam: North-Holland Publishing Co.

Chao, Yuen-Ren. 1920. A system of tone-letters. *Le Maître phonétique* 45:24-27.

Chen, Matthew. 1970. Vowel length variation as a function of the voicing of the consonant environment. *Phonetica* 22:129-59.

Chinebuah, I. K. 1962. A phonetic and phonological study of the nominal piece in Nzima. Master's thesis, University of London. Cited in Abercrombie (1967) but not seen.

Chomsky, Noam, and Morris Halle. 1968. *The sound pattern of English*. New York: Harper and Row.

Conklin, H. C. 1949. Preliminary report on field work on the islands of Mindors and Palawan, Phillippines. *American Anthropologist* 51:268-73.

Davis, Irvine. 1962. Phonological function in Cheyenne. *International Journal of American Linguistics* 28:36-42.

Doke, C. M. 1931. *A comparative study in Shona phonetics*. Johannesburg: University of the Witwatersrand.

Dunstan, Elizabeth. 1964. Towards a phonology of Ngwe. *Journal of West African Languages* 1:39-42.

———— 1967. Tone and concord systems in Ngwe nominals. Doctoral thesis, University of London.

Ferguson, Charles A., Moukhter Ani, et al. 1961. *Damascus Arabic*. Washington: Center for Applied Linguistics.

Firth, J. R. 1957. *Papers in linguistics, 1934-1951*. London: Oxford University Press.

Foley, James. 1970a. Phonological distinctive features. *Folia Linguistica* 4:87-92.

———— 1970b. A systematic phonological interpretation of the Germanic consonant shifts. *Language Sciences* 9:11-12.

———— 1971. The English vowel shift. *Glossa* 4, no. 2. In press.

Gleason, Henry A. 1961. Review of African language studies I. *Language* 37:294-308.

Greenberg, Joseph. 1970. Some generalizations concerning glottalic consonants, especially implosives. *International Journal of American Linguistics* 36:123-45.

Guthrie, Malcolm. 1948. *The classification of the Bantu languages.* London: Oxford University Press.

Halle, Morris, and K. N. Stevens. 1971. A note on laryngeal features. Quarterly Progress Report of the Research Laboratory of Electronics 101:198-213. Massachusetts Institute of Technology.

Hamp, Eric. 1958. On Comanche voiceless vowels. *International Journal of American Linguistics* 24:321-22.

Heffner, R-M. S. 1950. *General phonetics.* Madison: University of Wisconsin Press.

Hockett, Charles F. 1955. *A manual of phonology.* Indiana University Publications in Anthropology and Linguistics, memoir 11. Baltimore: Waverly Press. Also published as part 1 of *International Journal of American Linguistics* vol. 21, no. 4.

Hoffman, Carl. 1963. *A grammar of the Margi language.* London: Oxford University Press.

Hudgins, C. V., and R. H. Stetson. 1935. Voicing of consonants by depression of the larynx. *Archives néerlandaises de phonétique expérimentale* 11:1-28.

Hyman, Larry M. 1970. How concrete is phonology? *Language* 46:58-76.

International Phonetic Association. 1949. *Principles of the International Phonetic Association.* Revised edition. London: International Phonetic Association.

Jakobson, Roman. 1962. *Selected writings I: Phonological studies.* The Hague: Mouton.

Jakobson, Roman, C. Gunnar M. Fant, and Morris Halle. 1952. *Preliminaries to speech analysis: The distinctive features and their correlates.* Massachusetts Institute of Technology Acoustics Laboratories Technical Report, no. 13.

Jakobson, Roman, and Morris Halle. 1956. *Fundamentals of language.* Janua Linguarum 1. The Hague: Mouton.

———— 1964. Tenseness and laxness. In *In honour of Daniel Jones,* edited by David Abercrombie, D. B. Fry, P. A. D. MacCarthy, N. C. Scott, and J. L. M. Trim, pp. 96-101. London: Longmans.

Johnson, Jeanette. 1966. Tamazight phonology. Unpublished paper, University of California, Los Angeles.

Jones, Daniel. 1956. *An outline of English phonetics.* 8th edition. Cambridge: Heffer.

114

Jones, S. 1929. Radiography and pronunciation. *British Journal of Radiology* 2, no. 15:149-56.

Kelly, John. 1966. A note on lip-rounding. *Le Maître phonétique* 125:8-9.

Kent, R. D., and K. L. Moll. 1969. Vocal-tract characteristics of the stop cognates. *Journal of the Acoustical Society of America* 46:1549-55.

Kenyon, John S., and Thomas A. Knott. 1953. *A pronouncing dictionary of American English.* Springfield, Mass.: G. & C. Merriam.

Kim, Chin-Wu. 1965. On the autonomy of the tensity feature in stop classification. *Word* 21:339-59.

——— 1970. A theory of aspiration. *Phonetica* 21:107-16.

Klatt, D. H., K. N. Stevens, and J. Mead. 1968. Studies of articulatory activity and airflow during speech. In *Sound production in man,* edited by Arend Bouhuys, pp. 42-55. Annals of the New York Academy of Sciences, vol. 155, art. 1.

Kozhevnikov, V. A., and L. A. Chistovich, editors. 1965. *Speech: Articulation and perception.* Translated, and available as JPRS 30,543. Washington: Department of Commerce.

Labov, William D. 1971. The internal evolution of linguistic rules. In *Linguistic change and generative theory: Essays from the UCLA conference on historical linguistics in the perspective of transformational theory, February 1969.* Edited by Robert P. Stockwell and Ronald K. S. Macauley. Bloomington: Indiana University Press. Forthcoming.

Ladefoged, Peter. 1957. Use of palatography. *Journal of Speech and Hearing Disorders* 22:764-74.

——— 1958. Syllables and stress. *Miscellanea Phonetica* 3:1-14.

——— 1962. *Elements of acoustic phonetics.* Chicago: University of Chicago Press.

——— 1963. Some physiological parameters in speech. *Language and Speech* 6:109-19.

——— 1964a. *A phonetic study of West African languages.* Cambridge: Cambridge University Press.

——— 1964b. Some possibilities in speech synthesis. *Language and Speech* 7:205-14.

——— 1965. The nature of general phonetic theories. Georgetown University Monograph Series on Languages and Linguistics, no. 18. Edited by Charles W. Kreidler, pp. 27-42. Washington: Georgetown University Press.

——— 1967. *Three areas of experimental phonetics.* London: Oxford University Press.

——— 1968. Linguistic aspects of respiratory phenomena. In *Sound production in man,* edited by Arend Bouhuys, pp. 141-51. Annals of the New York Academy of Sciences, vol. 155, art. 1.

———— 1970. The measurement of phonetic similarity. *Statistical Methods in Linguistics* 6:23-32 (Språkförlaget Skriptor, Stockholm).

———— 1971*a*. Phonetic prerequisites for a distinctive feature theory. In *Melange á la mémoire de Pierre Delattre*, edited by Albert Valdman. The Hague: Mouton. Forthcoming.

———— 1971*b*. The limits of phonology. In *Form and substance*, edited by Børge Spang-Thomsen, pp. 47-56. Copenhagen: Akademisk Forlag. Forthcoming.

Lanham, L. W. 1964. The proliferation and extension of Bantu phonemic systems influenced by Bushman and Hottentot. In *Proceedings of the Ninth International Congress of Linguists,* edited by H. Lunt, pp. 382-90. The Hague: Mouton.

Lees, Robert. 1961. *The phonology of modern Turkish*. Bloomington: Indiana University Press.

Lehiste, Ilse. 1964. *Acoustical characteristics of selected English consonants*. Indiana University Research Center in Anthropology, Folklore, and Linguistics, publication 34. Bloomington: Indiana University Press; The Hague: Mouton. Also published as part 4 of *International Journal of American Linguistics* vol 30, no. 3.

Lehiste, Ilse, and Gordon Peterson. 1961. Some basic considerations in the analysis of intonation. *Journal of the Acoustical Society of America* 33:419-25.

Lieberman, Phillip. 1960. Some acoustic correlates of word stress in American English. *Journal of the Acoustical Society of America* 32:451-54.

———— 1967. *Intonation, perception, and language*. Research Monograph Series, no. 38. Cambridge: MIT Press.

Lindblom, Bjorn. 1968. Temporal organization of syllable production. Speech Transmission Laboratory Quarterly Progress and Status Report 2-3(1968):1-6. Royal Institute of Technology (KTH), Stockholm.

Lindblom, Bjorn, and Johan Sundberg. 1969. A quantitative theory of cardinal vowels and the teaching of pronunciation. Speech Transmission Laboratory Quarterly Progress and Status Report 2-3(1969):19-25. Royal Institute of Technology (KTH), Stockholm.

Lisker, Leigh, and Arthur S. Abramson. 1964. A cross-language study of voicing in initial stops: Acoustical measurements. *Word* 20:384-422.

———— 1967. Some effects of context on voice onset time in English stops. *Language and Speech* 10:1-28.

Malmberg, Bertil. 1956. Distinctive features of Swedish vowels, some instrumental and structural data. In *For Roman Jakobson*, edited by Morris Halle, pp. 316-21. The Hague: Mouton.

Merrifield, William R. 1963. Palantla Chinantec syllable types. *Anthropological Linguistics* 5, no. 5:1-16.

Moll, Kenneth L., and T. H. Shriner. 1967. Preliminary investigation of a new concept of velar activity during speech. *The Cleft Palate Journal* 4:58-69.

Moore, Paul, and Hans von Leden. 1958. Dynamic variations of the vibratory pattern of the normal larynx. *Folia Phoniatrica* 10:205-38.

Netsell, R. 1969. Subglottal and intraoral air pressures during the intervocalic contrast of /t/ and /d/. *Phonetica* 20:68-73.

———— 1970. Underlying physiological mechanisms of syllable stress. *Journal of the Acoustical Society of America* 470:103-4.

Ohala, John. 1970. Aspects of the control and production of speech. Working Papers in Phonetics 15. University of California, Los Angeles.

Öhman, Sven. 1967. Word and sentence intonation: A quantitative model. Speech Transmission Laboratory Quarterly Progress and Status Report 2-3(1967):20-54. Royal Institute of Technology (KTH), Stockholm.

Pandit, P. B. 1957. Nasalisation, aspiration and murmur in Gujarati. *Indian Linguistics* 17:165-72.

Perkell, Joseph S. 1965. Cineradiographic studies of speech: Implications of a detailed analysis of certain articulatory movements. *Proceedings of the Fifth International Congress of Acoustics*, vol. 1a, paper A32. Université de Liège.

———— 1969. *Physiology of speech production: Results and implications of a quantitative cineradiographic study.* Research Monograph Series, no. 53. Cambridge: MIT Press.

Peterson, Gordon, and June Shoup. 1966. A physiological theory of phonetics. *Journal of Speech and Hearing Research* 9:6-67.

Pike, Eunice V. 1963. *Dictation exercises in phonetics.* Glendale: Summer Institute of Linguistics.

Pike, Kenneth L. 1943. *Phonetics.* University of Michigan Publication in Language and Literature, vol. 21.

———— 1948. *Tone languages:* Ann Arbor: University of Michigan Press.

Schachter, Paul. 1961. Phonetic similarity in tonemic analysis. *Language* 37:321-39.

Shipley, William F. 1953. *Maidu texts and dictionary.* University of California Publications on Linguistics 33. Berkeley and Los Angeles: University of California Press.

———— 1964. *Maidu grammar.* University of California Publications on Linguistics 41. Berkeley and Los Angeles: University of California Press.

Smith, K. D. 1968. Laryngealization and delaryngealization in Sedang phonemics. *Linguistics* 38:52-69.

Smith, Timothy S. 1971. A phonetic study of the function of the extrinsic tongue muscles. Working Papers in Phonetics 18. University of California, Los Angeles.

Stevens, Kenneth N., and Arthur House. 1955. Development of a quantitative description of vowel articulation. *Journal of the Acoustical Society of America* 27:484-93.

Sweet, Henry. 1890. *A primer of phonetics*. Oxford: The Clarendon Press.

Tucker, A. N. 1940. *The Eastern Sudanic languages*. London: Oxford University Press.

Tucker, A. N., and Margaret Bryan. 1966. *Linguistic analyses: The non-Bantu languages of North Eastern Africa*. London: Oxford University Press.

Vanderslice, Ralph. 1968. Synthetic elocution: Considerations in automatic orthographic-to-phonetic conversion of English with special reference to prosodic features. Working Papers in Phonetics 8. University of California, Los Angeles.

Wang, William. 1967. Phonological features of tone. *International Journal of American Linguistics* 33:93-105.

Welmers, William. 1959. Tonemics, morphotonemics, and tonal morphemes. *General Linguistics* 4:1-9.

Westermann, D., and Ida Ward. 1933. *Practical phonetics for students of African languages*. London: Oxford University Press.

Whiteley, Wilfred H., and M. G. Muli. 1962. *Practical introduction to Kamba*. London: Oxford University Press.

Williams, Ann F., and Eunice V. Pike. 1968. The phonology of Western Popoloca. *Lingua* 20:368-80.

Subject Index

Language Index

Bold type indicates that data reported in the text on those languages is from my own investigations.

Consonant Chart

	Bilabial	Labio-dental	Dental & Alveolar	Retroflex	Palato-alveolar	Palatal	Velar	Labial-velar	Uvular	Pharyngeal	Glottal
Nasal	m		n	ɳ		ɲ	ŋ	ŋ͡m	N		
Plosives	p b		t d	ʈ ɖ		c ɟ	k g k͡p g͡b q ɢ				ʔ
Implosives	ɓ		ɗ			ɠ					
Ejectives	pʼ		tʼ			kʼ					
(Central) Fricative	ɸ β	f v	θ ð / s z	ʂ ʐ	ʃ ʒ	ç ʝ̂	x ɣ ʍ ŵ		χ ʁ	ħ ʕ	
Lateral Fricative			ɬ ɮ								
(Central) Approximant	ʋ		ɹ	ɻ		j	w	ʁ			h
Lateral (Approximant)			l	ɭ		ʎ					
Trill			r						R		
Tap			ɾ								
Flap				ɽ							

Diacritics

Voiceless	˳	n̥	Dental	˷	t̪
Aspirated	ʰ	tʰ	Labialized	ʷ	tʷ
Murmured	¨	b̤	Palatalized	ʲ	tʲ
Laryngealized	˜	b̰	Nasalized	˜	w̃ ẽ
Raised	˄	w̭	Long	ː	nː
Lowered	˅	θ̬	Half long	·	n·
Retracted	˃	t̠	Syllabic	ˎ	n̩
Advanced	˂	t̪	Velarized or pharyngealized	˜	z̴ ɫ